The Welcome Table
Planning Masses with Children

Elizabeth McMahon Jeep

with

Robert W. Hovda

Gabe Huck

Robert H. Oldershaw

Meg Reisett

Joyce Schemanske

Edited by Mary Ann Simcoe

LTP

Acknowledgments

Many of the selections presented here originally appeared in other publications. We gratefully acknowledge the following publishers.

Peter Li, Inc. for the following articles by Elizabeth McMahon Jeep that appeared in *Catechist* magazine:

"Community Planning for Community Prayer," adapted from the articles, "Community Planning for Community Prayer" © February 1979 and "A Good Beginning" © September 1979.

"The Student Liturgy Committee," adapted from the articles, "Thoughts on Themes" © October 1978 and "To Build a Tower" © September 1980.

"Themes or Themesong?" © February 1981.

" 'W-A-T-E-R' " © October 1980.

"Meditation at a Pack Meeting" © January 1982.

"Going Somewhere?" © January 1979.

"The Story Gift" © October 1981.

"Children and Ministries" © February 1982.

"The Liturgy and 'Memorizable' Prayers" © May 1981.

The Liturgical Conference for selections from *Signs, Songs and Stories: Another Look at Children's Liturgies* © 1974 by The Liturgical Conference, Inc.:

"How Children Grow" by Meg Reisett.

"Putting the Pieces Together" by Robert W. Hovda.

The English translation of the *Directory for Masses with Children* © 1973, International Committee on English in the Liturgy, Inc. All rights reserved.

Portions of "Copyrights and Wrongs" are taken from *Copyright: The United States Copyright Law, a Guide for Church Musicians*, produced by the Church Music Publishers Association. No copyright is claimed in this publication.

The following articles by Elizabeth McMahon Jeep originally appeared in *Liturgy 80* in the series "In My Father's House: Reflections for the Leader of Children's Liturgy":

"There Was a Time."

"Getting to Know You."

"The Priest as Storyteller."

"Homilies for Children."

Cover and artwork by Suzanne M. Novak

Designed by Michael Tapia

ISBN 0-930467-38-8

Contents

Introduction

The Welcome Table: Planning Masses with Children is primarily for classroom teachers, catechists and priests—those adults who are often expected to know how to celebrate the Mass with children. For classroom teachers, planning a celebration of Mass is often one more preparation for which there is too little time and too little guidance. Catechists in religious education programs usually have even less time to prepare children for the celebration; and, because the celebration of Mass with these students is infrequent, catechists feel the demand of providing a quality celebration all the more. The clergy, who preside at Mass with every conceivable subgroup of the parish community, sometimes find celebrating Mass with children like praying in a strange tongue.

For these, *The Welcome Table* combines insight and practical suggestions for planning the celebration of Mass with children. Many aids for ''children's liturgies'' emphasize formulas for this undertaking: orders of worship, songs to sing, themes to announce, homilies to preach and activities for the children. They make liturgy preparation something like planning a lesson. Despite introductions that may urge readers to adapt the material, busy adults often use these plans wholesale.

This book does not provide ideas for Masses with children in ''lesson plan'' format. *The Welcome Table* is shaped by the conviction that the art of planning Masses with children begins with allowing children to meet the liturgy in the company of adult Christians who know and respect both the needs of children and the dynamics of the liturgy.

First, the children. Adult liturgy planners must know and appreciate children. Teachers, catechists and priests who do, know that children move, and sing (and move), and ask questions (and move), and make noise (and move), and sometimes have startlingly clear insights into faith and life.

In order for children to participate in the Mass, their age and abilities must be taken into account. To help adult liturgy planners work and pray with children, we include an overview of children's development, a model for student liturgy committees, and reflections for presiders and the adult assembly on their attitudes toward the presence of children in the worshiping assembly.

Next, there is the Mass with its own way of ordering things—its own language of word and ritual, music and silence, greetings and dialogues, gestures and processions, structure and spontaneity. Before they can make prudent judgments about how to celebrate Mass with children, adults who plan liturgies must have a working knowledge of how the Mass is put together. The section, "Understanding the Mass," is devoted to the structure of the Mass, the eucharistic prayers for Masses with children, and a detailed chart for understanding and planning the Mass. The section, "The Language of Liturgy," offers insight into various elements of ritual—music, movement, storytelling, ministries—with suggestions for introducing this special language to children.

Finally, there is the art of putting children and liturgy together. In this the church is not without guidance. The *Directory for Masses with Children* and three eucharistic prayers for Masses with children, promulgated by the Congregation for Divine Worship in 1973 and 1974 respectively, provide the standards against which all Masses with children must be measured. The *Directory* provides principles for introducing young Catholics to the liturgical life of the church and guidelines for celebrating Mass with them. The *Directory* is so fundamental a document that it is included here as preliminary reading. Even those familiar with it should read it one more time.

This book, too, is written under the judgment of the *Directory for Masses with Children*. *The Welcome Table* does not address the entire spectrum of initiating children into the liturgical life of the church. The *Directory* clearly states that participation in noneucharistic celebrations "plays a major role in the liturgical formation of children." *The Welcome Table* addresses the Mass only. The *Directory* distinguishes between two common situations in which children are present at Mass: the usual parish eucharistic assembly on Sundays and holydays with many adults and fewer children; and those Masses with a group of children for which few adults are present. This book is addressed only to the latter occasion, an assembly composed primarily of children.

The adults who will read and use *The Welcome Table* have the wonderful and awesome responsibility of handing on the living tradition of faith to the next generation. They are to lead our children to the table in ways that respect and promote our children's faith now and for the future. They must see to it that celebrations with children are worthy of our liturgical tradition. This book is offered with the hope that bringing children to our common table will be a welcome responsibility for the adults who accompany them, and that the invitation to the table will be welcomed by our children.

—*Mary Ann Simcoe*

I. Our Children's Future

There Was a Time

— Elizabeth McMahon Jeep

There was a time when our children came to church knowing what to expect and how to follow the ceremonies. They knew all about blessings and litanies and saints' days. They knew the arithmetic of liturgical cycles and seasons and colors. Today we are lucky if they know the difference between a reading and a petition! As the French liturgist Joseph Gelineau says: we have within a single generation moved from christendom to the diaspora, from a world that accepted religious values and initiated children into the language as part of a total cultural package to a believing minority scattered in an alien society. Even in areas where Catholicism still enjoys a numerical dominance, we find ourselves teaching children the liturgy as if it were a foreign language.

The home is no longer a school of liturgical prayer; the word of God is seldom read to children there, and only remnants of religious rituals survive. The family meal is little appreciated as a sacramental encounter— indeed, it is hardly seen as important enough to fight for.

A larger and larger percentage of our children who go to public schools receive their religious instruction in an evening or on the weekend. In that setting there is little leisure

for liturgical experience. Teachers often lack training in the development of prayer forms, and what singing is done is usually of catechetical rather than liturgical music.

Even in Catholic schools the teachers do not always understand the dynamic of liturgical prayer and may resort to the three-hymns-and-a-banner approach for planning a school eucharist. There is often an absence of the liturgical dimension in the daily school prayer and a failure to build continuity between daily prayer and Sunday worship.

The church is genuinely concerned about this situation. In 1973 a *Directory for Masses with Children* was issued. The introduction states, "It cannot be expected that everything in the liturgy will always be intelligible to [children]. Nonetheless, we may fear spiritual harm if over the years children repeatedly experience in the church things that are scarcely comprehensible to them. . . ." (DMC #2) With that in mind, the Congregation for Divine Worship outlined a very flexible guide for those who are responsible for the liturgical initiation of children. This *Directory* was followed in 1974 by the approval of three eucharistic prayers for Masses with children, and in 1980 the United States Catholic Conference published two musical settings for each of those eucharistic prayers. In addition to these documents and prayers, there have been a number of workshops and publications

ELIZABETH MCMAHON JEEP is a noted catechist and the author of a number of books on religious education, liturgy and the family.

on children's liturgy offered by official and unofficial sources across the country.

The church, in other words, has tried to give support and direction to the improvement of children's worship. And what direction is pointed out to us? In general, the church seems to be saying that the renewal of children's liturgy (like the renewal of liturgy for adults) can only come about through the establishment of *community* and the return to *simplicity*.

Children and Adults Together

If, then, children come to the liturgy for the most part as visitors to a foreign land, what can we do to make their stay agreeable and fruitful? We must first find out whether or not they know one another. Where the culture does not reinforce one's faith, the believing group among whom one lives and those whom one knows by name assume a greater significance. The assembly is vital. Liturgy presumes community; it can enhance but not create community. We cannot celebrate some aspect of our life together if we do not in fact have a life together.

A sense of community depends in part on sharing a task. Do our children feel responsible for the liturgy they celebrate? Is it theirs or their teacher's? Have they gotten the idea that liturgy is a passive experience? According to a national survey conducted by the Bishop's Committee on the Liturgy (*BCL Report*, no. 1) only nine percent of the parishes in the nation include students at planning sessions for their own liturgies. Our liturgies, it seems, share some similarities with children's theater where plays are produced *for* children *by* adults. In the theater certain techniques are used to lessen the psychological and actual distance between the performers and audience, such as having the actors enter and exit from the aisles rather than the wings, but there is no doubt that the children are there as interested observers rather than active participants.

Perhaps other examples of cooperation between adults and children can offer a variety of models for interaction and shared responsibility. At a birthday party, for example, the child-host is a member of the planning team and has significant input regarding the guest list, games and food: the adult offers suggestions, helps evaluate alternatives, and maintains veto power and budget control; the child-guests bring gifts, join the games and songs, eat, and enter into the spirit of the occasion.

Community athletic teams offer another example. The child-volunteers and their parents realize that no one wins games without coaching, practice, enthusiasm, and a sense of responsibility to the team on the part of both the players and the adults who support them; the children learn as much during the game as they do during the practice; practices continue no matter how good the team is for its league.

Adults give children a sense of recognition and accomplishment. There are many parallels here that might help us see children's liturgy in a wider context, yet one should not stretch comparisons beyond their usefulness. There is nothing exactly like the liturgy.

Worship, Pure and Simple

The striking thing about other forms of activity between adults and children is the way in which complex operations can be accommodated to a wide range of ages and skill levels. An essential, perhaps *the* essential ingredient seems to be the ability of adults to identify the basic elements of the activity for the children, and help them to master those. For example, no one starts off a group of would-be Reggie Jacksons with descriptions of bunts, triple plays and scoring systems. Rather, with a ball and a bat, the children learn to swing, hit, run and catch. That is an appropriate and sufficient beginning. Those basics will allow the youngsters to play a game with one another without damaging undeveloped pitching muscles or becoming so lost in refinements that they are bored or scared away. Gradually, interest and skill can develop.

Simplicity is the watchword! Simplicity and clarity are the essential characteristics for any activity in which adults wish to engage children. If the liturgy is a celebration of faith and at the same time a renewal and nourishment of that faith, we should be able to simplify and adapt our rubrics for children, so that they can step into the circle and join the dance. There must be a simple first step in the initiation process that is lifelong and community-wide. This is what we are urged to by the *Directory for Masses with Children:* it is not a matter of creating an entirely separate "kiddie-liturgy" but of "retaining, shortening, or omitting some elements or of making a better selection of texts" (#3); catechesis on the Mass "should be directed to the child's active, conscious, and authentic participation" (#12); "various kinds of celebrations" (i.e. non-eucharistic) should be introduced (#13); celebrations "should avoid having too didactic a character" (#13); leaders should "take great care that the children do not feel neglected" (#17); "as many children as possible should have special parts" (#22); planners should "avoid any excess of rites" (#40). Thus the document describes both the *attitude* the priest and the community should have toward child-believers, and the *latitude* within which suitable services can be developed for them.

It is an enlightening exercise to read the *Directory* and mark up a missalette, scratching out everything that can be eliminated and reducing the essential parts to their simplest possible form. What you have left is surprisingly spare. It is the beginning, the space within which we can be creative and responsible to the needs of children. It is the foundation from which we and the children can gradually build celebrations that are true expressions of the faith of the Christian community and true expressions of the lives and prayer of the children participating. With that "core curriculum" in hand, we cannot help but read with dismay the report of the American bishops that among those parishes where special Masses for children are offered 34 percent rarely or never use a dialogue homily, 85 percent use the maximum number of readings, 30 percent rarely or never omit or abbreviate elements of the introductory rite, 23 percent rarely or never adapt or reword the prayers and invitations.

We are obviously misunderstanding or simply ignoring the import of the church's teaching on children and liturgy. Where do we go from here? As a beginning, the liturgy planners and clergy can read and discuss the *Directory* in order to deepen their own competence and develop a common understanding of their task. Next the group can weigh the needs and practices within the parish and draw up a list of goals and priorities from which long- and short-range strategies can be developed. It is simply a matter of identifying where you want to go and deciding how you are going to get there. It requires the cooperation of all those who have a role to play in the development of children's liturgies. It requires the ability to think beyond the writing of petitions for next Wednesday's eucharist. It requires us to think about the liturgical attitudes and skills we want our children to have when they become mature in the faith and practices of the Catholic community.

Directory for Masses with Children

The Directory for Masses with Children *is a refreshing document. We often skip over official documents, sure that they will be dry and heavy reading. But this document is different. That is why it is part of this book's text and not an appendix to be referred to at leisure. The* Directory *is essential reading for those who want to enrich children's worship. It is official encouragement to do what our best sense tells us must be done—to celebrate the Mass in ways that help our children pray it well.*

A pastoral document, the Directory *is a response to the "repeated petitions of the entire Catholic world" for guidance in helping children participate in the liturgy in ways "suited to their age." A practical document, the* Directory *sets the scope for adapting the Mass for children and provides concrete suggestions for planners.*

But the Directory*'s sights go far beyond adjustments in the order of Mass: children's ability to celebrate the liturgy depends on far more. It relies on quite human capacities—the ability to listen, to gather around the family table, to greet one another in friendship. Learning to pray the liturgy is fostered by living in a Christian home, the witness of a parish community, the whole of Christian formation. Our children must be told the gospel stories many times, led in simple prayer ceremonies and taught our songs of praise.*

The Directory for Masses with Children *is concerned with all the ways of initiating children into full and active participation in the liturgical life of the church. This breadth of perspective is combined with very practical guidelines; therein lies the genius of this document.* —EDITOR

Introduction

(1) The Church shows special concern for baptized children who have yet to be fully initiated through the sacraments of confirmation and eucharist as well as for children who have only recently been admitted to holy communion. Today the circumstances in which children grow up are not favorable to their spiritual progress.[1] In addition, sometimes parents barely fulfill the obligations of Christian education which they undertake at the baptism of their children.

(2) In bringing up children in the Church a special difficulty arises from the fact that liturgical celebrations, especially the eucharist, cannot fully exercise their innate pedagogical force upon children.[2] Although the mother tongue may now be used at Mass, still the words and signs have not been sufficiently adapted to the capacity of children.

In fact, even in daily life children cannot always understand everything that they experience with adults, and they easily become weary. It cannot be expected, moreover, that everything in the liturgy will always be intelligible to them. Nonetheless, we may fear spiritual harm if over the years children repeatedly experience in the Church things that are scarcely comprehensible to them: recent psychological study has established how profoundly children are formed by the religious experience of infancy and early childhood, according to their individual religious capacity.[3]

(3) The Church follows its Master, who "put his arms around the children . . . and blessed them" (Mark 10:16). It cannot leave children to themselves. The Second Vatican Council had spoken in the Constitution on the Liturgy about the need for liturgical adaptations for various groups.[4] Soon afterwards, especially in the first Synod of Bishops held in Rome in 1967, the Church began to consider how participation of children could be made easier. On the occasion of the Synod the president of the Consilium for the Implementation of the Constitution on the Liturgy said explicitly that it could not be a matter of "creating some entirely special rite but rather of retaining, shortening, or omitting some elements or of making a better selection of texts."[5]

(4) All the details of eucharistic celebrations with a congregation were determined in the General Instruction of the revised *Roman Missal*, published in 1969. Then this congregation began to prepare a special directory for Masses with children, as a supplement to the instruction. This was done in response to repeated petitions from the entire Catholic world and with the cooperation of men and women specialists from almost every nation.

(5) Like the General Instruction, this directory reserves some adaptations to conferences of bishops and individual bishops.[6]

With regard to adaptations of the Mass which may be necessary for children in a given country but which cannot be included in this general directory, the conferences of bishops should submit proposals to the Apostolic See, in accord with article 40 of the Constitution on the Liturgy. These adaptations are to be introduced only with the consent of the Apostolic See.

(6) The directory is concerned with children who have not yet entered the period of pre-adolescence. It does not speak directly of children who are physically or mentally retarded because a broader adaptation is sometimes necessary for them.[7] Nevertheless, the following norms may also be applied to the retarded, with the necessary changes.

(7) The first chapter of the directory (#8-15) gives a kind of foundation by considering the different ways in which children are introduced to the eucharistic liturgy. The second chapter briefly treats Masses with adults, in which children also take part (#16-19). Finally, the third chapter (#20-54) treats at greater length Masses with children, in which only some adults take part.

I. The Introduction of Children to the Eucharistic Celebration

(8) A fully Christian life cannot be conceived without participation in the liturgical services in which the faithful, gathered into a single assembly, celebrate the paschal mystery. Therefore, the religious initiation of children must be in harmony with this purpose.[8] By baptizing infants, the Church expresses its confidence in the gifts received from this sacrament; thus it must be concerned that the baptized grow in communion with Christ and the brethren. Sharing in the eucharist is the sign and pledge of this very communion. Children are prepared for eucharistic communion and introduced more deeply into

its meaning. It is not right to separate such liturgical and eucharistic formation from the general human and Christian education of children. Indeed it would be harmful if liturgical formation lacked such a foundation.

(9) For this reason all who have a part in the formation of children should consult and work together. In this way even if children already have some feeling for God and the things of God, they may also experience the human values which are found in the eucharistic celebration, depending upon their age and personal progress. These values are the activity of the community, exchange of greetings, capacity to listen and to seek and grant pardon, expression of gratitude, experience of symbolic actions, a meal of friendship, and festive celebration.[9]

Eucharistic catechesis, which is mentioned in #12, should go beyond such human values. Thus, depending on their age, psychological condition, and social situation, children may gradually open their minds to the perception of Christian values and the celebration of the mystery of Christ.[10]

(10) The Christian family has the greatest role in teaching these Christian and human values.[11] Thus Christian education, provided by parents and other educators, should be strongly encouraged in relation to liturgical formation of children as well.

By reason of the responsibility freely accepted at the baptism of their children, parents are bound in conscience to teach them gradually to pray. This they do by praying with them each day and by introducing them to prayers said privately.[12] If children are prepared in this way, even from their early years, and do take part in the Mass with their family when they wish, they will easily begin to sing and to pray in the liturgical community, indeed they will have some kind of foretaste of the eucharistic mystery.

If the parents are weak in faith but still wish their children to receive Christian formation, at least they should be urged to share the human values mentioned above with their children. On occasion, they should be encouraged to participate in meetings of parents and in non-eucharistic celebrations with their children.

(11) The Christian communities to which the individual families belong or in which the children live also have a responsibility toward children baptized in the Church. By giving witness to the Gospel, living fraternal charity, actively celebrating the mysteries of Christ, the Christian community is the best school of Christian and liturgical formation for the children who live in it.

Within the Christian community, godparents and others with special concern who are moved by apostolic zeal can help greatly in the necessary catechesis of children of families which are unable to fulfill their own responsibility in Christian education.

In particular these ends can be served by preschool programs, Catholic schools, and various kinds of classes for children.

(12) Even in the case of children, the liturgy itself always exerts its own proper didactic force.[13] Yet within programs of catechetical, scholastic, and parochial formation, the necessary importance should be given to catechesis on the Mass.[14] This catechesis should be directed to the child's active, conscious, and authentic participation.[15] "Clearly accommodated to the age and mentality of the children, it should attempt, through the principal rites and prayers, to convey the meaning of the Mass, including a participation in the whole life of the Church."[16] This is especially true of the text of the eucharistic prayer and of the acclamations with which the children take part in this prayer.

Special mention should be made of the catechesis through which children are prepared for first communion. Not only should they learn the truths of faith concerning the eucharist, but they should also understand how from first communion on—prepared by penance according to their need and fully initiated into the body of Christ—they may actively participate in the eucharist with the people of God and have their place at the

Lord's table and in the community of the brethren.

(13) Various kinds of celebrations may also play a major role in the liturgical formation of children and in their preparation for the Church's liturgical life. By the very fact of celebration children easily come to appreciate some liturgical elements, for example, greetings, silence, and common praise (especially when this is sung in common). Such celebrations, however, should avoid having too didactic a character.

(14) Depending on the capacity of the children, the word of God should have a greater and greater place in these celebrations. In fact, as the spiritual capacity of children develops, celebrations of the word of God in the strict sense should be held frequently, especially during Advent and Lent.[17] These will help greatly to develop in the children an appreciation of the word of God.

(15) Over and above what has been said already, all liturgical and eucharistic formation should be directed toward a greater and greater response to the Gospel in the daily life of the children.

II. Masses with Adults in which Children Also Participate

(16) Parish Masses are celebrated in many places, especially on Sundays and holydays, with a large number of adults and a smaller number of children. On such occasions the witness of adult believers can have a great effect upon the children. Adults can also benefit spiritually from experiencing the part which the children have within the Christian community. If children take part in these Masses together with their parents and other members of their family, this should be of great help to the Christian spirit of families.

Infants who as yet are unable or unwilling to take part in the Mass may be brought in at the end of Mass to be blessed together with the rest of the community. This may be done, for example, if parish helpers have been taking care of them in a separate area.

(17) Nevertheless, in Masses of this kind it is necessary to take great care that the children do not feel neglected because of their inability to participate or to understand what happens and what is proclaimed in the celebration. Some account should be taken of their presence, for example, by speaking to them directly in the introductory comments (as at the beginning and the end of Mass) and in part of the homily.

Sometimes, moreover, it will perhaps be appropriate, if the physical arrangements and the circumstances of the community permit, to celebrate the liturgy of the word, including a homily, with the children in a separate area that is not too far removed. Then, before the eucharistic liturgy begins, the children are led to the place where the adults have meanwhile been celebrating their own liturgy of the word.

(18) It may also be very helpful to give some tasks to the children. They may, for example, bring forward the gifts or sing one or other of the parts of Mass.

(19) Sometimes, if the number of children is large, it may be suitable to plan the Masses so that they correspond better to the needs of the children. In this case the homily should be directed to the children but in such a way that adults may also benefit from it. In addition to the adaptations now in the Order of Mass, one or other of the special adaptations described below may be employed in a Mass celebrated with adults in which children also participate, where the bishop permits such adaptations.

III. Masses with Children in which Only a Few Adults Participate

(20) In addition to the Masses in which children take part with their parents and other members of their family (which are not always possible everywhere), Masses with children in which only some adults take part are recommended, especially during the week. From the beginning of the liturgical restoration it has been clear to everyone that some adaptations are necessary in these Masses.[18]

Such adaptations, but only those of a more general kind, will be considered below (#38–54).

(21) It is always necessary to keep in mind that through these eucharistic celebrations children must be led toward the celebration of Mass with adults, especially the Masses in which the Christian community comes together on Sundays.[19] Thus, apart from adaptations which are necessary because of the children's age, the result should not be entirely special rites which differ too greatly from the Order of Mass celebrated with a congregation.[20] The purpose of the various elements should always correspond with what is said in the General Instruction of the *Roman Missal* on individual points, even if at times for pastoral reasons an absolute *identity* cannot be insisted upon.

Offices and Ministries in the Celebration

(22) The principles of active and conscious participation are in a sense even more valid for Masses celebrated with children. Every effort should be made to increase this participation and to make it more intense. For this reason as many children as possible should have special parts in the celebration, for example: preparing the place and the altar (see #29), acting as cantor (see #24), singing in a choir, playing musical instruments (see #32), proclaiming the readings (see #24 and 47), responding during the homily (see #48), reciting the intentions of the general intercessions, bringing the gifts to the altar, and performing similar activities in accord with the usage of various communities (see #34).

To encourage participation it will sometimes be helpful to have several additions, for example, the insertion of motives for giving thanks before the priest begins the dialogue of the preface.

In all this one should keep in mind that external activities will be fruitless and even harmful if they do not serve the internal participation of the children. Thus religious silence has its importance even in Masses with children (see #37). The children should not be allowed to forget that all the forms of participation reach their high point in eucharistic communion when the body and blood of Christ are received as spiritual nourishment.[21]

(23) It is the responsibility of the priest who celebrates with children to make the celebration festive, fraternal, meditative.[22] Even more than in Masses with adults, the priest should try to bring about this kind of spirit. It will depend upon his personal preparation and his manner of acting and speaking with others.

Above all, the priest should be concerned about the dignity, clarity, and simplicity of his actions and gestures. In speaking to the children he should express himself so that he will be easily understood, while avoiding any childish style of speech.

The free use of introductory comments[23] will lead children to a genuine liturgical participation, but these explanations should not be merely didactic.

It will help in reaching the hearts of the children if the priest sometimes uses his own words when he gives invitations, for example, at the penitential rite, the prayer over the gifts, the Lord's Prayer, the sign of peace, and communion.

(24) Since the eucharist is always the action of the entire Church community, the participation of at least some adults is desirable. These should be present not as monitors but as participants, praying with the children and helping them to the extent necessary.

With the consent of the pastor or the rector of the church, one of the adults may speak to the children after the gospel, especially if the priest finds it difficult to adapt himself to the mentality of the children. In this matter the norms of the Congregation for the Clergy should be observed.

The diversity of ministries should also be encouraged in Masses with children so that the Mass may be evidently the celebration of a community.[24] For example, readers and cantors, whether children or adults, should be employed. In this way variety will keep the children from becoming tired because of the sameness of voices.

Place and Time of Celebration

(25) The primary place for the eucharistic celebration for children is the church. Within the church, however, a space should be carefully chosen, if available, which will be suited to the number of participants. It should be a place where the children can conduct themselves freely according to the demands of a living liturgy that is suited to their age.

If the church does not satisfy these demands, it will sometimes be suitable to celebrate the eucharist with children outside a sacred place. Then the place chosen should be appropriate and worthy.[25]

(26) The time of day chosen for Masses with children should correspond with the circumstances of their lives so that they may be most open to hearing the word of God and to celebrating the eucharist.

(27) Weekday Mass in which children participate can certainly be celebrated with greater effect and less danger of weariness if it does not take place every day (for example, in boarding schools). Moreover, preparation can be more careful if there is a longer interval between celebrations.

Sometimes it is preferable to have common prayer to which the children may contribute spontaneously, either a common meditation or a celebration of the word of God. These celebrations continue the eucharist and lead to deeper participation in later eucharistic celebrations.

(28) When the number of children who celebrate the eucharist together is very great,

attentive and conscious participation becomes more difficult. Therefore, if possible, several groups should be formed; these should not be set up rigidly according to age but with regard to the progress of religious formation and catechetical preparation of the children.

During the week such groups may be invited to the sacrifice of the Mass on different days.

Preparation for the Celebration

(29) Each eucharistic celebration with children should be carefully prepared beforehand, especially with regard to prayers, songs, readings, and intentions of the general intercessions. This should be done in discussion with the adults and with the children who will have a special ministry in these Masses. If possible, some of the children should take part in preparing and ornamenting the place of celebration and preparing the chalice with the paten and the cruets. Over and above the appropriate internal participation, such activity will help to develop the spirit of community celebration.

Singing and Music

(30) Singing is of great importance in all celebrations, but it is to be especially encouraged in every way for Masses celebrated with children, in view of their special affinity for music.[26] The culture of various groups and the capabilities of the children present should be taken into account.

If possible the acclamations should be sung by the children rather than recited, especially the acclamations which are a part of the eucharistic prayer.

(31) To facilitate the children's participation in singing the Gloria, profession of faith, Sanctus, and Agnus Dei, it is permissible to use music set to appropriate vernacular texts, accepted by the competent authority, even if these do not agree completely with the liturgical texts.[27]

(32) The use of "musical instruments may be of great help" in Masses with children, especially if they are played by the children

themselves.[28] The playing of instruments will help to support the singing or to encourage the reflection of the children; sometimes by themselves instruments express festive joy and the praise of God.

Care should always be taken, however, that the music does not prevail over the singing or become a distraction rather than a help to the children. Music should correspond to the purpose which is attached to the different periods for which it is introduced into the Mass.

With these precautions and with special and necessary concern, music that is technically produced may be also used in Masses with children, in accord with norms established by the conferences of bishops.

Gestures and Actions

(33) The development of gestures, postures, and actions is very important for Masses with children in view of the nature of the liturgy as an activity of the entire man and in view of the psychology of children. This should be done in harmony with the age and local usage. Much depends not only on the actions of the priest,[29] but also on the manner in which the children conduct themselves as a community.

If a conference of bishops, in accord with the norm of the General Instruction of the *Roman Missal,*[30] adapts the actions of the Mass to the mentality of the people, it should give consideration to the special condition of children or should determine such adaptations for children only.

(34) Among the actions which are considered under this heading, processions deserve special mention as do other activities which involve physical participation.

The processional entrance of the children with the priest may help them to experience a sense of the communion that is thus constituted.[31] The participation of at least some children in the procession with the book of gospels makes clear the presence of Christ who announces his word to the people. The procession of children with the chalice and the gifts expresses clearly the value and meaning of

the preparation of gifts. The communion procession, if properly arranged, helps greatly to develop the piety of the children.

Visual Elements

(35) The liturgy of the Mass contains many visual elements, and these should be given great prominence with children. This is especially true of the particular visual elements in the course of the liturgical year, for example, the veneration of the cross, the Easter candle, the lights on the feast of the Presentation of the Lord, and the variety of colors and liturgical ornaments.

In addition to the visual elements that belong to the celebration and to the place of celebration, it is appropriate to introduce other elements which will permit children to perceive visually the great deeds of God in creation and redemption and thus support their prayer. The liturgy should never appear as something dry and merely intellectual.

(36) For the same reason the use of pictures prepared by the children themselves may be useful, for example, to illustrate a homily, to give a visual dimension to the intentions of the general intercessions, or to inspire reflection.

Silence

(37) Even in Masses with children "silence should be observed at the proper times as a part of the celebration"[32] lest too great a role be given to external action. In their own way children are genuinely capable of reflection. They need, however, a kind of introduction so that they will learn how to reflect within themselves, meditate briefly, or praise God and pray to him in their hearts[33] for example after the homily or after communion.[34]

Besides this, with even greater care than in Masses with adults, the liturgical texts should be spoken intelligibly and unhurriedly, with the necessary pauses.

The Parts of Mass

(38) The general structure of the Mass, which "in some sense consists of two parts, namely, the liturgy of the word and the liturgy of the

eucharist,'' should always be maintained as should some rites to open and conclude the celebration.[35] Within individual parts of the celebration the adaptations which follow seem necessary if children are truly to experience, in their own way and according to the psychological patterns of childhood, "the mystery of faith . . . by means of rites and prayers.''[36]

(39) Some rites and texts should never be adapted for children lest the difference between Masses with children and the Masses with adults become too great.[37] These are "the acclamations and the responses of the faithful to the greetings of the priest,''[38] the Lord's Prayer, and the trinitarian formula at the end of the blessing with which the priest concludes the Mass. It is urged, moreover, that children should become accustomed to the Nicene Creed little by little, while the use of the Apostles' Creed mentioned in #49 is permitted.

A. Introductory Rite
(40) The introductory rite of Mass has the purpose "that the faithful, assembling in unity, should constitute a communion and should prepare themselves properly for hearing the word of God and celebrating the eucharist worthily.''[39] Therefore every effort should be made to create this disposition in the children and to avoid any excess of rites in this part of Mass.

It is sometimes proper to omit one or other element of the introductory rite or perhaps to enlarge one of the elements. There should always be at least some introductory element, which is completed by the opening prayer or collect. In choosing individual elements one should be careful that each one be used at times and that none be entirely neglected.

B. Reading and Explanation
of the Word of God
(41) Since readings taken from holy scripture constitute "the principal part of the liturgy of the word,''[40] biblical reading should never be omitted even in Masses celebrated with children.

(42) With regard to the number of readings on Sundays and feast days, the decrees of the conference of bishops should be observed. If three or even two readings on Sundays or weekdays can be understood by children only with difficulty, it is permissible to read two or only one of them, but the reading of the gospel should never be omitted.

(43) If all the readings assigned to the day seem to be unsuited to the capacity of the children, it is permissible to choose readings or a reading either from the *Lectionary for Mass* or directly from the Bible, taking into account the liturgical seasons. It is urged, moreover, that the individual conferences of bishops prepare lectionaries for Masses with children.

If because of the limited capabilities of the children it seems necessary to omit one or other verse of a biblical reading, this should be done cautiously and in such a way "that the meaning of the texts or the sense and, as it were, style of the scriptures are not mutilated.''[41]

(44) In the choice of readings the criterion to be followed is the quality rather than the quantity of the texts from the scriptures. In itself a shorter reading is not always more suited to children than a lengthy reading. Everything depends upon the spiritual advantage which the reading can offer to children.

(45) In the biblical texts "God speaks to his people . . . and Christ himself is present through his word in the assembly of the faithful.''[42] Paraphrases of scripture should therefore be avoided. On the other hand, the use of translations which may already exist for the catechesis of children and which are accepted by the competent authority is recommended.

(46) Verses of psalms, carefully selected in accord with the understanding of children, or singing in the form of psalmody or the alleluia with a simple verse should be sung between the readings. The children should always have a part in this singing, but sometimes a reflective silence may be substituted for the singing.

If only a single reading is chosen, there may be singing after the homily.

(47) All the elements which will help to understand the readings should be given great consideration so that the children may make the biblical readings their own and may come more and more to appreciate the value of God's word.

Among these elements are the introductory comments which may precede the readings[43] and help the children to listen better and more fruitfully, either by explaining the context or by introducing the text itself. In interpreting and illustrating the readings from the scriptures in the Mass on a saint's day, an account of the life of the saint may be given not only in the homily but even before the readings in the form of a commentary.

Where the text of the readings suggest, it may be helpful to have the children read it with parts distributed among them, as is provided for the reading of the Lord's Passion during Holy Week.

(48) The homily in which the word of God is unfolded should be given great prominence in all Masses with children. Sometimes the homily intended for children should become a dialogue with them, unless it is preferred that they should listen in silence.

(49) If the profession of faith occurs at the end of the liturgy of the word, the Apostles' Creed may be used with children, especially because it is part of their catechetical formation.

C. Presidential Prayer

(50) The priest is permitted to choose from the *Roman Missal* texts of presidential prayers more suited to children, keeping in mind the liturgical season, so that he may truly associate the children with himself.

(51) Sometimes this principle of selection is insufficient if the children are to consider the prayers as the expression of their own lives and their own religious experience, since the prayers were composed for adult Christians.[44] In this case the text of prayers of the *Roman Missal*

may be adapted to the needs of children, but this should be done in such a way that, preserving the purpose of the prayer and to some extent its substance as well, the priest avoids anything that is foreign to the literary genre of a presidential prayer, such as moral exhortations or a childish manner of speech.

(52) The eucharistic prayer is of the greatest importance in the eucharist celebrated with children because it is the high point of the entire celebration.[45] Much depends upon the manner in which the priest proclaims this prayer[46] and in which the children take part by listening and making their acclamations.

The disposition of mind required for this central part of the celebration, the calm and reverence with which everything is done, should make the children as attentive as possible. They should be attentive to the real presence of Christ on the altar under the species of bread and wine, to his offering, to the thanksgiving through him and with him and in him, and to the offering of the Church which is made during the prayer and by which the faithful offer themselves and their lives with Christ to the eternal Father in the Holy Sprit.

For the present, the four eucharistic prayers approved by the supreme authority for Masses with adults are to be employed and kept in liturgical use until the Apostolic See makes other provision for Masses with children.

D. Rites before Communion

(53) At the end of the eucharistic prayer, the Lord's Prayer, the breaking of the bread, and the invitation to communion should always follow.[47] These elements have the principal significance in the structure of this part of the Mass.

E. Communion and the Following Rites

(54) Everything should be done so that the children who are properly disposed and who have already been admitted to the eucharist may go to the holy table calmly and with recollection, so that they may take part fully in the eucharistic mystery. If possible there should

be singing, accommodated to the understanding of children, during the communion procession.[48]

The invitation which precedes the final blessing[49] is important in Masses with children. Before they are dismissed they need some repetition and application of what they heard, but this should be done in a very few words. In particular, this is the appropriate time to express the connection between the liturgy and life.

At least sometimes, depending on the liturgical seasons and the different circumstances in the life of the children, the priest should use the richer forms of blessing, but he should always retain the trinitarian formula with the sign of the cross at the end.[50]

(55) The contents of the directory are intended to help children quickly and joyfully to encounter Christ together in the eucharistic celebration and to stand in the presence of the Father with him.[51] If they are formed by conscious and active participation in the eucharistic sacrifice and meal, they should learn day by day, at home and away from home, to proclaim Christ to others among their family and among their peers, by living the "faith, which expresses itself through love" (Galatians 5:6).

This directory was prepared by the Congregation for Divine Worship. On October 22, 1973, the Supreme Pontiff, Paul VI, approved and confirmed it and ordered that it be made public.

From the office of the Congregation for Divine Worship, November 1, 1973, the solemnity of All Saints.

Notes

1. See Congregation for the Clergy, *Directorium Catechisticum Generale*, #5, *AAS*, 64 (1972) 101–102.

2. See Vatican Council II, Constitution on the Liturgy, *Sacrosanctum Concilium*, #33.

3. See DCG 78: *AAS*, 64 (1972) 146–147.

4. See CL 38; also Congregation for Divine Worship, instruction *Actio pastoralis*, May 15, 1969: *AAS*, 61 (1969) 806–811.

5. First Synod of Bishops, Liturgy: *Notitiae*, 3 (1967) 368.

6. See below, #19, 32, 33.

7. See Order of Mass with children who are deafmutes for German-speaking countries, confirmed June 26, 1970, by this congregation (prot. no. 1546/70).

8. See CL 14, 19.

9. See DCG 25: *AAS*, 64 (1972) 114.

10. See Vatican Council II, Declaration on Christian Education, *Gravissimum educationis,* #2.

11. See *Ibid.*, 3.

12. See DCG 78: *AAS*, 64 (1972) 147.

13. See CL 33.

14. See Congregation of Rites, instruction *Eucharisticum mysterium*, May 25, 1967, #14: *AAS*, 59 (1967) 550.

15. See DCG 25: *AAS*, 64 (1972) 114.

16. See EM 14: *AAS*, 59 (1967) 550; also DCG 57; *AAS*: 64 (1972) 131.

17. See CL 35, 4.

18. See above, #3.

19. See CL 42, 106.

20. See first Synod of Bishops, Liturgy: *Notitiae*, 3 (1967) 368.

21. See General Instruction of the Roman Missal, #56.

22. See below, #37.

23. See GI 11.

24. See CL 28.

25. See GI 253.

26. See GI 19.

27. See Congregation of Rites, instruction *Musicam sacram*, March 5, 1967, #55: *AAS*, 59 (1967) 316.

28. *Ibid.*, 62: *AAS*, 59 (1967) 318.

29. See above, #23.

30. See GI 21.

31. See GI 24.

32. See GI 23.

33. See EM, #38: *AAS*, 59 (1967) 562.

34. See GI 23.

35. See GI 8.

36. See CL 48.

37. See above, #21.

38. GI 15.

39. GI 24.

40. GI 38.

41. See *Lectionary for Mass*, introduction, #7d.

42. GI 33.

43. See GI 11.

44. See Consilium for the Implementation of the Constitution on the Liturgy, Instruction on Translation of Liturgical Texts, January 25, 1969, #20: *Notitiae*, 5 (1969) 7.

45. See GI 54.

46. See above, #23, 37.

47. See above, #23.

48. See instruction *Musicam sacram,* #32: *AAS*, 59 (1967) 309.

49. See GI 11.

50. See above, #19.

51. See Eucharistic Prayer II.

II. Working with Children

How Children Grow

— Meg Reisett

All adults who work with children must know how to provide their youngsters with opportunities to move forward toward maturity. Leaders of children's liturgy groups are no exception. If liturgy is a celebration of life—life transformed, made new in the Lord Jesus—it certainly must aid and enhance life's natural changes.

What brings about the changes in children's feelings, actions and growth that we call development? Nobody really knows. As a result of several decades of scientific study of children, we now have access to some facts and many theories. Quite a few mysteries remain.

This summary of children's needs and development is based on the assumption that personal growth is a complicated interweaving of biology and experience. Biology provides each child with some inner drives, with genetic codes for growth, with the sense avenues for acquiring information about the world.

Experience provides the stimuli which "turn on" the biological child. Experience includes affection, intellectual stimulation, nutrition, praise and criticism, color and texture, security and threats, bicycles and television, and all the other happenings in a person's life. Without experience, there is no activation of the child's mind and body.

At each period in a child's life there are certain problems or tasks that must be

MEG REISETT is professionally trained in Montessori methods and human development.

mastered if the growth toward maturity is going to continue. These "developmental tasks" result from the interaction of biological changes and the demands of experience and culture. For infants, there are developmental tasks such as learning to walk, talk, control elimination, etc. In this section we will be describing the tasks for six- to twelve-year-old children.

Physical Changes

Physically, six-year-old children have come a long way. They've learned to control their movements so that such complicated phenomena as walking, running, talking, drawing, throwing are now old habits. They've managed to control their bodily functions and have learned to recognize and react to the signs of fatigue, hunger, thirst and pain.

After six years of rapid growth, the child's body takes on a more even course in height and weight gain. There are some spurts of change here and there over the years, just a reminder that the dramatic onset of puberty is on the way.

After six or so years devoted to basic muscle mastery, a child's energies are now devoted to refinement. If Janie knows how to draw, she wants to learn more and more complex pictures. If Jeff knows how to run, he wants to learn the complicated running needed for soccer. You've seen the six-year-old's struggle with printing the alphabet. You've seen the hours spent on jump-rope games. You've seen the devotion to the basketball and net. All of these events are witness to the beautiful determination of each child to make the body serve as a tool for thinking, curiosity, social needs.

The developmental tasks of physical growth include:

- improving the skill and control of large muscles;
- learning the skills required for organized games and sports;
- gaining control of fine muscle movements;
- developing physical prowess and athletic skills.

Work with children in liturgies must allow them to work on their developmental tasks in some way.

Intellectual Growth

In the earliest years of thinking, a child learns that objects have permanence—that the teddy bear doesn't cease to exist when the baby can no longer see it. Later, small children learn that objects serve as signs for other things or events or ideas. Toddlers know that when mother picks up the car keys, it means a trip to the store or the park. It is characteristic of young children to judge all events by their appearances; a three-year-old may say that the steam shovel eats the dirt. Also, young children are almost completely egocentric. All of these characteristics of thinking are totally natural for children under six or so years.

At about the age of six or seven a child's thinking makes a big leap toward maturity. The "age of reason" it is called. The late Swiss psychologist Jean Piaget, who thoroughly described children's thinking, called the years from seven to eleven "the stage of concrete operations." Now the child's thinking becomes increasingly logical and systematic. When children encounter a situation which they cannot deal with because of lack of experience, they are able to use analogy as a tool.

Youngsters are able to understand that objects are not essentially changed just because they change in size or shape or color or some other appearance.

These children now begin to realize that words do not have the power of action, that words are not the same as things, that "saying doesn't make it so." (How often you hear the phrase, "Sticks and stones can break my bones but words can never hurt me!")

Children in these elementary years can make and work with mental images, they can plan, they can predict what will happen if. . . . They can organize what they know about the world and understand complex series of events, symbol systems, causes and effects. Now they can think through a problem without having to "rehearse it" or act it out. They are more consistent, more logical and much more like adults in their thinking processes.

The developmental tasks of intellectual growth include:

- learning the symbol systems (numbers, letters, reading, computing) as required by our culture;
- learning, understanding, recognizing the physical phenomena of the world;
- developing skills of memory, analogy, logic, problem-solving, creative thinking, abstraction.

Work with children in liturgies must allow them to work on their developmental tasks in some way.

Social and Emotional Growth

In the beginning a baby's entire emotional world is circumscribed by the persons who provide nourishment. If a baby's needs for food, warmth, physical contact, stimulation and comfort are met in a sure, predictable manner, trust is learned. On this foundation of trust (or lack of it) will be developed all other patterns for emotional growth and personal relationships. Gradually children learn to relate to persons other than their "nourishers"—relatives, friends, babysitters, teachers. Self-esteem grows and falters continually, and is especially critical at about age five, when the "oedipal crisis" occurs. At this point in their emotional growth, boys and girls, each in their own way, must resolve their feelings of love and possessiveness for their opposite-sex parent. As a result of resolving the problem successfully, boys learn to identify with their fathers, girls with their mothers. If the crisis isn't completely resolved, children can be left with strong feelings of inferiority.

Children of six or so years must have many opportunities to combat this sense of inadequacy by learning more and more about what they *can* do. In the same way a baby needs sucking, school-age children need to work, to be challenged to do things. Another way for a child to develop a sense of adequacy (or sense of industry, as Erik Erikson calls it) is by identifying with adults who are adequate— adults who *know* many things, and who *know how to do* many things. It is also critical for children to experience success. When a boy sees evidence of his accomplishment in a woodworking class, there can be no doubt about his adequacy. When a girl learns to ride her bike or to rollerskate, she need not worry so much about her inferiority.

Socially, the years from six on are most decisive. In younger years, each child's values were determined primarily by the family. But now the peer group plays an ever more important role, and huge amounts of energy are devoted to gaining acceptance and recognition from classmates and friends. The problems of dependency, of security, of giving and taking love were once the struggles of home. Now they are worked out on the playground, in the classroom, in clubs and cliques and gangs. The code of the group becomes ever more important.

Another critical emotional event during the years from six to twelve is each child's acceptance of his or her sex role in society. These years are called the "latency period," not because emotions are missing, but because the strong surges of feelings are more dormant than before—sort of a lull before the storm of puberty. But during this "quiet time" boys and girls work on accepting themselves as male and female. They investigate the roles society gives to men and women, and start to fit those roles into their own expectations for themselves.

The developmental tasks for emotional growth include:

- developing a sense of industry, leaving behind the feelings of inferiority;
- developing friendships outside the family circle and achieving a degree of independence from family;
- gaining acceptance and prestige from the peer group;
- finding constructive ways of dealing with frustrations, threats, anger, fear;
- learning and accepting the appropriate sex role.

Work with children in liturgies must allow them to work on their developmental tasks in some way.

Ways of Working on the Developmental Tasks

The chart that follows presents some *do*s and *don't*s, practical hints to make it easier for you to meet children's needs while planning and celebrating special liturgies which involve them.

Ways of Working on Developmental Tasks

Do	Don't	Comments
Do allow for lots of talking, especially in the planning times.	Don't do too much talking yourself.	Children need to tell you, and each other, about themselves and about their lives. They use talking to explain, and also to solve their problems. In the very process of saying what happened or how it felt, a child can come to greater self-acceptance and understanding.
Do use many and varied forms of expression.	Don't get stuck in the pattern of using only word and song.	Children need to explore with all of their muscles, all their senses. Are you really satisfied to use only the eyes, the ears and the vocal chords? What about tastes and smells? What about mime, acrobatics or modern dance? What about costumes, lighting effects, sound effects? What about body rhythms, body strength, the joy of moving in unison with other bodies?
Do find each child's area of success.	Don't expect all the children to be good at everything.	Point out Joyce's good singing voice, Sherman's skill at making posters, Beverly's ease with cartwheels, Jeff's ability to understand how other kids are feeling. Appreciate the variety of gifts among children, and encourage them to share your appreciation.
Do answer children's questions, no matter how silly or out of context they may seem.	Don't make children feel foolish or "bad" because of their curiosity.	There is a lot that young boys and girls don't know about their feelings and their bodies, about what happens during illness, about death, about God, about the rules of society, about why and when and how and where. You must share with them what you know, and give them the opportunity to use that tool we call knowledge.
Do allow the children to love you.	Don't make them dependent on you.	Children, like all of us, need to love and be loved. They need love in the form of trust, acceptance, limits, challenges, encouragement. We don't honor their growth needs by making ourselves the focal point for affection or the source of all favors.
Do expect children to learn from each other.	Don't expect to be their only source of values and information.	Remember, during these years peers become ever more important.
Do realize that what children want most of all is to be accepted.	Don't sentimentalize childhood as the "wonderful, enchanting, golden years."	Children, like the rest of us, also know moments of loneliness, boredom, fear and hostility. If they learn from us to understand and accept all their feelings, they will have the best chance for constant self-esteem.
Do allow (within limits) for frivolity, play and exploration.	Don't be overly serious and product-oriented.	The process by which you and the children develop celebrations can itself be a celebration of growth.

Community Planning for Community Prayer

— Elizabeth McMahon Jeep

A visit to the exhibit booths at a religious educators' convention is always a mixed blessing. There is the pleasure of inspecting new materials, and running into friends one has not seen since the last convention, but there is also the frustration of seeing people buy second-rate materials.

It is especially discouraging to see the continued popularity of "instant liturgies" for children. One book of them goes so far as to offer homilies for the celebrant to read! What ever happened to that tried but true educational maxim: Learn by doing. Surely it applies to liturgy as well as to arithmetic! The teacher who cannot construct a simple classroom prayer ritual will never adequately communicate the dynamics of liturgy to students, and students who do not learn to plan liturgies may never experience the profoundly personal meaning that worship can hold.

There is, of course, a need to stimulate one's imagination and deepen one's theological insight—many books offer helpful ideas. It is the TV dinner approach to ready-made liturgies which is self-defeating. One simple resolution can reduce teachers' reliance on ready-made plans when it is time to prepare the liturgy for children. Repeat after me: *This year I will absolutely and positively give the children a larger role in developing their own liturgies!*

Giving up "instant liturgies" for student-planned liturgies involves a basic attitude and sensitivity toward liturgy as well as the children with whom we celebrate. Why should children be drawn (gradually, and in ways appropriate to their age) into the planning of liturgies which they will celebrate? Here are just a few of the dozen or more reasons.

- It will give them a greater sense of ownership and responsibility for a celebration if they are involved more actively in the preparation.

- Children know better than the teacher or pastor what is on their minds that is worth praying about. They apply a given season or reading to their lives in often surprising ways. The conversations which student committees hold when trying to select readings or songs help to clarify, at least for those on the committee, the purpose of the liturgy—the *reason* for prayer. The teacher who listens to these discussions may discover unexpected flashes of maturity—and of ignorance— in the children.

- The generation of adults of which these students will be a part will take a greater responsibility for all aspects of church life, including the planning and ministries of divine worship. The liturgy of the future, which these children will help to create, depends upon the liturgical formation which the children receive now.

- Accepting a creative role in any endeavor helps to build a healthy sense of self-confidence. Playing a creative role in the church fosters a sense of Christian self-identity and responsibility. Each person who has received the water of baptism and the chrism of confirmation should recognize in himself or herself a responsible agent in the church, not just a receiver, a consumer of religious services.

- Working with the liturgy deepens one's taste for worship as well as one's talent for it. It is possible for all children to experience the behind-the-scenes workings of the service, whether it is the Easter Vigil or a simple classroom ceremony. A generation ago only preadolescent boys, in their role as acolytes, were allowed this privilege.

- It is important that children, as well as adults, carry their personal and communal experience of God through the whole process of worship. The presence of God, experienced as the motive of prayer, must be allowed to find expression in the design and preparation of a liturgy and participation in that liturgy. Out of students' attempts to express what is in their hearts through the liturgy will grow a continually maturing experience of the church, which no book of ''instant liturgies'' can hope to produce.

Two Examples

Let us use a hypothetical example to see just where a resolution to involve children responsibly in planning liturgies would lead. At the beginning of every school year, parochial schools all across the country gather their children to celebrate that grand old tradition, the opening Mass. This ritual beginning and dedication of the fresh new school year is one of the very few liturgies designed to celebrate an event of significance to children's lives.

Planning for this event at the parish of St. Prisca-the-Practical went like this: the faculty took 30 minutes of their September meeting to choose the date, readings (Votive Mass of the Holy Spirit), ministries (eighth grade supplies acolytes, seventh grade readers, sixth grade prayers of petition, etc.), visuals (red antependium saved from Pentecost—with a flame and the words ''fill us with the fire of your love''), offertory gifts (textbooks symbolizing the work of the year). The religion department chairperson will brief the celebrant and write a dedication of the school year for use before the final blessing. The music teacher will select and rehearse appropriate hymns. All religion teachers will spend at least two class periods discussing the indwelling of the Holy Spirit, with reference in the lower grades to Pentecost and in the upper grades to confirmation. The result—a liturgy that is coherent, if overly theological. It does, however, bear the marks of something created by adults. Can you imagine children coming up with the idea of carrying textbooks in the procession?

Meanwhile, at the adjoining parish of St. Cora-the-Creative the religion department chairperson has met with the 16 members of the liturgy committee (two delegates from each grade) for lunch every day for a week. During their 45 minutes over bag lunches they have talked about how they feel toward the new school year (scared, excited, disappointed, and, for the eighth graders, powerful); agreed that the phrase ''growing up'' best expressed their ideas (rejecting ''beginnings,'' ''new year'' and ''courage''); identified possible readings (the finding of Jesus in the temple—he was growing up faster than his parents realized, and the agony in the garden—Jesus needed courage to face what was coming); designed an activity to help all students prepare themselves for the liturgy (during religion class each child will make a list of the things he or she likes or dreads about school, then save the list to put in a large vase during the entrance procession.

(Yes, the *whole school* takes part in the procession!); and divided up the jobs, i.e., explaining the preparations to each classroom, ministries, meeting with the celebrant, acting out the gospel of the finding of Jesus in the temple. They decided against any special visuals. They selected favorite music from last year—a gospel alleluia, acclamations for the eucharistic prayer and two hymns.

The result—a liturgy clearly related to children's experience of the opening of the school year. It bears the fingerprints of its student origins: each part has its own logic but the whole lacks a certain unity.

No one can say that either of these liturgies could engage the attention of every student, but St. Cora's can at least guarantee 16 fully involved children, and that may be as much as we can ever hope for.

No Excuses

Student involvement in planning the liturgies they will celebrate is a project often begun and abandoned. The reasons are often the same. We tried but it failed. The children got bored. Their ideas were too far out. They spent the whole meeting discussing and never made any decisions. Meetings took too much time. No one was willing to be moderator. It is more efficient for the principal to assign a task to each grade.

Before abandoning this goal once again, admit that it will not be any easier to form a student liturgy committee after "things settle down a bit"; things never settle down until classes are out in June. It will always be faster, easier and more efficient to assign tasks to students rather than to invite them to choices.

Admit that execution of someone else's plans (the teacher's or the "instant liturgy's"), no matter how excellent the plans, will *never* create the sense of involvement and responsibility that the planners experience.

Admit that liturgy planning, like walking, is a learned skill. The learning requires instruction, practice, self-confidence and the opportunity to make lots of mistakes. It is also, like walking, simple enough for a child to learn.

And, one more time, repeat after me: *This year I will absolutely and positively give the children a larger role in developing their own liturgies!*

The Student Liturgy Committee

— Elizabeth McMahon Jeep

"Would any of you think of building a tower without first sitting down and calculating the cost, to see whether you could afford to finish it?" Jesus asked the question first and the church asks it again whenever this gospel is proclaimed. The gospel urges us to clarify our goals before we begin, so that we can realistically estimate the costs of achieving them and our willingness to pay the price. Otherwise, we will abandon our project and as the gospel warns, "everyone then will laugh and say, 'There is the one who started to build and could not finish!'"

Beginning a student liturgy committee takes the same sort of careful assessment. What makes a children's liturgy committee work? How is it organized? I offer one model that has been effective. Try it. Adapt it to your parish or school.

Every liturgy committee must begin with a moderator—a good listener who works well with children and has a solid background in liturgy (including the *Directory for Masses with Children*). This moderator can be a priest, but will more often be the religious education director, principal or religion teacher. Next add two students from each middle and upper level class—grades four to eight. If each liturgy has its own moderator and committee, no one is overburdened and several committees can be meeting simultaneously. Parish school students can meet during a study period or lunch break two or three times per week as needed. Just ask

them to bring their lunches to a designated table in the cafeteria or, better, to a room without distraction. CCD students will have to meet during regular class, which could be extended if parents are not inconvenienced.

The moderator convokes the meeting and, without any preliminary speeches, announces the assignment (e.g., "We must plan a school eucharist for All Saints Day.") and the guidelines (e.g., "We want only two readings.").

Then comes the first task—to "break open" the meaning of the feast. The children need to discover in it something concrete and personal to celebrate. The planning committee will therefore begin by sorting through what they already know of the feast, by reading and discussing the scripture passages (when the readings for the day are prescribed by the lectionary), and asking what the feast means in terms of real life: "What does *sanctity* mean? How can we tell who is holy? What does a saint do for us?" The moderator keeps the conversation on the point, brisk but not rushed.

This activity should unearth many possible directions to pursue, since the scriptures are so rich and their various liturgical settings so suggestive. The adult notes the meanings that surface, listens for possible images that can express that meaning and continues questioning the committee in order to push their thinking beyond dry theology to statements of personal meaning. For example, the children might begin to talk about the saints as *living in heaven*. The moderator will steer them away from fantasies of a fairy-tale heaven by asking: "What would a city of saints be like? What changes would you expect to see in *our* city if all the saints came here to live?"

When several valid ideas or images have been introduced, the moderator forms them into simple sentences (e.g., Saints are heroes for us to imitate. Saints build a city of peace and justice.) and asks the children to choose *one*. The most difficult task is not digging out *some* focus for the celebration, but selecting *one* which is clearly relevant to the children, then suppressing the rest. That statement, written down and posted, shows the children that they have already accomplished something concrete, refreshes their memories at future planning sessions and prevents the moderator from "improving" upon it between meetings.

There are limitations to the use of this statement. It is *not* to be used to turn the liturgy into a lesson. In fact, the statement should ordinarily never be used within the liturgy itself. It is only a focusing device and must never rob the liturgy of its richness which simply cannot be summarized in words.

Without this essential process of reflection and discussion, liturgical planning is a matter of selecting elements that "we like" rather than those that can express the reality we are celebrating. It may take time for children to learn that the moderator is not playing the game of "keep talking and I will let you know when you discover the right answer." Confidence in their own insights will build.

Once this process has taken place, planning becomes a matter of marshaling visual, ritual and verbal elements which catch the spirit of the feast. The committee can think in terms of (a) something to see (poster, vestment, candle, etc.), (b) something to do (rituals, dances, processions, etc.), (c) something to say or sing (acclamations, responses, intercessions, etc.). This ABC approach is more satisfactory for young children than a step-by-step through-the-rubrics process. It also highlights the concern of the *Directory* that the elements of music, gesture, action, visuals and silence be given priority at liturgies with children.

During this phase the moderator must help the children avoid unrealistic plans. Then it only remains for the committee to prepare the community to celebrate.

Remember we are not reinventing the Mass. The planning process is not a substitute for a well established pattern of celebrating the eucharist according to the Roman rite under the guidance of the *Directory*. The goal is to have a strong, simple ritual where emphasis will always be on the fundamental actions that surround word and eucharist. When the children celebrate, this ritual pattern can be enhanced by the sights, actions and sounds of a feast or season.

The major steps and phases in liturgical planning (when the readings are prescribed by the lectionary) are:

1. a thoughtful examination of the readings and season or feast;

2. selection of a clear and pertinent focus which is relevant to the children;

3. application of that examination and focus to the liturgy;

4. preparation of the community, the ministers and the place of worship.

Step 3 may involve the elimination of at least one reading, slight editing of the readings or prayers and adaptation of some of the rites. These changes, which require sensitivity to the needs of the children and the rites of the church, are called for by the *Directory*. Refer to it for guidance in this area.

If each step of the process is kept simple, the experience should be a positive one for all, and worship within the student community will be enhanced. You should find as much satisfaction in the building of the tower as in its completion.

Themes or Themesong?

— Elizabeth McMahon Jeep

Initiation is the word of the moment in religious education circles. Yesterday it was *evangelization*, the day before *reconciliation*, and somewhere along the line there was a "Children's Year," a "Woman's Year" and a "Year of the Family." It is not always clear which of these come from Madison Avenue and which from Rome, but it does not seem to matter much. The strobe light of public attention rests briefly on some aspect of our lives and then passes. With the stroke of midnight, prayers and homilies on that theme cease, diocesan lesson plans are filed away, banners are removed from the sanctuary to make way for a new set. What will the theologians tell us to get excited about tomorrow?

It is a great shame that we do not draw more nourishment from these concerns. Perhaps, being Americans, we look upon them as simply part of our totally disposable, endlessly renewable environment. Disposable vestments, disposable liturgies, disposable themes, disposable theologies. Having been taught by Vatican II to expect change, perhaps we are relying on "them" (parish or school committees, diocesan commissions, bishops, popes, even the White House) to supply us with a steady stream of news releases suitable for celebrating in prayer and ritual.

Perhaps we have neglected the search for that which does not change, the personal search for the fundamental human meaning in our human experience. Let's be honest— sometimes we expect of a "theme" nothing more than that it make a children's liturgy enjoyable, much as we expect a lollipop to make a visit to the dentist tolerable. In those cases, it is not surprising that the "flavor" of the celebration lasts no longer than the flavor (artificial as it is!) of a lollipop.

If parish, school, religion class or family treat prayer in this way over the years, our children will be entertained or occupied, but their attention will have been drawn only to the surfaces of things, not to the inner, more universal realities those surfaces suggest. Above all, we will be scattering their attention rather than drawing it gradually deeper into the fundamental experience of the Christian community—eucharist, thanks-giving. That is the "theme" of every prayer, every ritual, every sacrament, every shout of "Abba" that the Holy Spirit inspires within us and among us. That is the Christian themesong, the recognizable melody woven through all of the movements of our communal opus, our life-symphony.

We don't create the themesong so much as we discover it. We discover it if we listen carefully, if we pay attention to the many sounds and phrases that make up our experience. We may hear it first from one side

28

of the orchestra, then from the other; now from the woodwinds, now from the piano, suddenly from the trumpets; each variation shaped by the instruments playing it and by the particular stage or mood of the movement.

In just this way, we listen to the sounds of life all around us and within us; from these sounds we compose the music of our prayer. If a theme, a concern, a theological point of view or parish preoccupation is presented to us as the subject for prayerful celebration we must be open to it. We must listen, ponder, test, observe, measure and validate it against our own experience and that of our community. We must study it and digest it and make it our own—integrate it into our symphony. We may be surprised to find that what we thought was merely the latest "theology of the month" is fresh, profound and lifegiving.

This is the service we can offer children. Their experiences are as real as ours, but their understanding of those experiences is not well modulated or integrated. We can help, *if* we are willing to listen. If we begin by listening—if we listen for a long time before we say anything—we will be less likely to end up with children's liturgies that are adult projects, that are lifeless or condescending, that are taken from a book of liturgy recipes, that are routinized, that only superficially involve the children.

Planning liturgy (and praying liturgically) is not easy. It requires a basic attitude as well as a method of approaching the actual design of a given prayer event. Like Christian life itself, it requires a clear head, capacity to hear and respond, openness to community, willingness to act in the absence of perfection, the desire to grow, the ability to play, the humanity to keep working on that symphony, listening to the music, and trying to get the notes just right.

III. The Language of Liturgy

"W-A-T-E-R"

— Elizabeth McMahon Jeep

On what would have been Helen Keller's one hundredth birthday, that remarkable woman was honored with speeches and ceremonies, a United States commemorative stamp, and an excellent new biography. It seems appropriate to give equal time to her remarkable teacher, Anne Sullivan.

Helen Keller was left blind and deaf by illness while she was still an infant. By the age of seven, she was almost uncontrollable, and her family was faced with the prospect of sending her to an institution. In desperation, they hired Anne Sullivan to try to civilize Helen, and, if possible, teach her sign language.

The struggle was long and the task seemed impossible, but one day Helen's world was transformed when her hand was held under a pump as Anne Sullivan spelled the word "water" into the other hand. Helen wrote, years later:

> Somehow the mystery of language was revealed to me. I knew that "w-a-t-e-r" meant the wonderful cool something that was flowing over my hand. That living word awakened my soul, gave it light, hope, joy, set it free! . . . Everything had a name, and each name gave birth to a new thought. As we returned to the house every object which I touched seemed to quiver with life. That was because I saw everything with the strange new sight that had come to me.

For Helen the word "water" became the word of life, the word of God itself. "Water" brought order into the chaos of her life, human contact with those around her, enabling her to learn who she was and who other people were. It allowed her to become an independent, thoughtful, self-directed person. "Water" enabled her to receive and express affection and meaning. It opened her to a world of love and security which had always surrounded her, but of which she had been unaware. The *word* was, for Helen, electrifying, life-giving, healing.

Catechists are very much like Anne Sullivan—carriers of the life-giving word of God to many students. We do not lay all our stress on *this* scripture or *that* ritual, *these* doctrines or *those* commandments. Such things do give shape to our teaching, but our real task is to lead each student to understand language itself—finally to realize and take the living word into his or her heart. The word itself, then, can draw the students on—as Helen Keller was led on—to a vision of the world and of their place in it.

Liturgy, too, is a language. Among other things it is a series of symbols used as a form of communication. As with any language, the symbols are more or less arbitrary, yet they embody meaning, reveal attitudes, make possible a sharing of feelings and vision, and act as a vehicle of conversation. Our task is to help children *learn the language* that is liturgy, not just parrot the words. The task requires patience and faith, and a bit of Anne Sullivan's method.

We have Helen Keller's own description of that method, in her story of the weeks which prepared her for the revelation at the water pump.

> When I played with [the toy] a little while, Miss Sullivan slowly spelled into my hand the word "d-o-l-l." I was at once interested in this finger play and tried to imitate it. When I finally succeeded in making the letters correctly, I was flushed with childish pleasure and pride. Running downstairs to my mother, I held up my hand and made the letters for doll. I did not know that I was spelling a word or even that words existed; I was simply making my fingers go in a monkey-like imitation. In the days that followed I learned to spell in this uncomprehending way a great many words.

In just this way our students sing the hymns we assign, and repeat our gestures of penitence, and recite uncomprehendingly the words of praise we teach them. They may enjoy the ceremonies, even as Helen enjoyed her spelling game, and still be untouched by the flow of the liturgical "conversation."

But this is not a cause for discouragement. As long as the liturgical "words" we spell into their hands reflect truly the realities of their lives, we can be confident that one day their eyes, too, will be opened, and they will suddenly discover that "everything has a name."

In the meantime, we stand by the pump like Anne Sullivan, letting the water flow over their hands. One day something will click, and the words we are spelling will become the living word. On that day our students will echo Helen's hymn of praise, "That living word awakened my soul, gave it light, hope, joy, set it free!"

Meditation at a Pack Meeting

— Elizabeth McMahon Jeep

The scoutmaster called for attention. The cub scouts and their families rose for the presentation of the colors. Four boys who were acting as color guard brought the flags to the center of the room and waited while we all recited the pledge of allegiance. They made quite a picture. One boy's shirt tail was hanging out; several boys were not in complete uniform; each was either showing off, giggling or signaling to friends—all seemed ill at ease. While I am not a strong advocate of the paramilitary dimension of the scout movement, it did seem to me that a little "spit and polish" would not have done those boys any harm. But even more than that, they needed a sense of place and a sense of ritual. They had not been prepared properly for their role in the public ceremony that was taking place. Indeed, it did not seem that anything more had been said to them than "When you are given a signal, get the flags, march from point X to point Y without falling down, and stand there until the pledge is over." My guess is that the ritual itself—its history and meaning—had never been explained to the boys. The adult leaders had simply presumed that they understood and respected the ancient custom.

It occurred to me then that catechists face a similar task in initiating children into the liturgical practices of a religious community. They must help the children understand, respect, and participate with poise in religious ceremonies.

Imperfect as our rituals are, they are nevertheless the time-honored ceremonies through which we express our faith and participate in the continuing life of Jesus and his church. The Sunday eucharist, the sacraments, the cycle of feasts and seasons— these liturgical events are actions of the church; they are moments of grace; they are a heritage that rightfully belongs to our children.

Catechists, then, form a bridge between these liturgical realities and the young Christians in their care. It is not an easy task in the best of times, but at the present, one of our greatest obstacles seems to be a cultural prejudice against formality. For some years our bubblegum and blue jean culture has emphasized slang and spontaneity, "telling it like it is" and "doing your own thing." In this atmosphere laziness, lack of preparation and lack of discipline on the part of the homilists, congregations, ministers or liturgy committees can be covered over with labels of "self-expression," "informality," and "boredom with irrelevant forms."

We must rescue liturgy from this silliness or risk losing an essential expression of our faith and source of growth as a church. We might begin by renewing our respect for formality. It is not the same as rigidity, or clericalism, or long faces or archaic language. It means rather that we all know what to expect, and that we are all able to move—without undue preliminaries—into the action of the celebration. Formality should not come from stiffness or distance but rather from a sense of dignity and peace. It should be a combination of the mutual respect the celebrants hold for one another, the attention that has been paid to preparing the environment and the ceremony, and the awareness of the continuing presence of God who has assembled the community in his name. That sort of formality is the mark of any prayerful community.

It is at the eucharist that our children learn to pray with the community. It is there that they see firsthand what it means for members of the community to assume various roles in the ceremony. It is there, Sunday after Sunday, year after year, that they experience the pace and variety and poise with which their adult friends lead and respond to elements of common prayer. In the classroom we can prepare them for this experience. We can help them design and celebrate small liturgies. We can help them become familiar with the history and meaning of Catholic ritual, we can help them become expert at various ministerial functions so that they understand liturgy as movement, and so that they will some day be able to step into these roles for the larger community. From a sense of competence comes poise and a sense of dignity.

"Formality" should carry the meaning of "giving form to" or "giving shape to." It connotes a pace, a plan, a process, a progress, appropriateness, dependability. The most informal birthday party has certain formalities, such as a cake, a birthday song or toast, gifts. Without those ritual elements it is just another party. Of course without the good spirits and affection of the guests and birthday person, the event would be *merely* a formality and no more.

Both form and spirit, body and soul are necessary for good public worship. It is necessary for good public liturgy of any kind—whether it is changing the guard at Buckingham Palace or presenting the colors to Wolf Pack 52; whether it is the installation of a new pope, or a call to prayer by the fifth grade CCD class.

Going Somewhere?

— Elizabeth McMahon Jeep

How can children be involved more deeply in the liturgy? Through action, movement, gesture? Children must pray as they do everything else, kinetically.

Processions are one of the easiest forms of movement to deal with, whether it is the uncomplicated march of several representatives with offertory gifts or the more general movement to and from communion. It does not take a great deal of planning or practice to turn a perfunctory or business-like walk from here to there into a dignified, even mood-setting action.

There are a number of ways, for example, in which a group of students might move from their seats to the ambo, lead the petitions of the faithful and return to their seats. In many cases the children are simply instructed to get there without giggling or tripping over one another, and the congregation interprets the time necessary for this "getting there" as a time-out in the liturgy. How different it is when the children form ranks of two as they leave their pews, walk slowly and gracefully to the altar, make a deep bow, turn and walk to the ambo—now their progress has become part of the prayer-action of the liturgy itself. The dignity of their bearing lends added weight to their words. The congregation has been brought along with them visually and shares in their sense of worship.

Some processions are minor, some are major; some involve one or several ministers, some allow for the participation of the entire community: but all require a sense of grace, pace and appropriateness. Regina Kuehn has said it well in *Liturgy 70* (February 1978):

> Processions are for people who move and who like to be moved, for people who have strong religious convictions and like to show them, for people who—by training, experience or intuition—know how much the body in its simple movement of walking does bring to the mind and to the spirit in fostering religious experience. Processions are for people who have a sense for symbolic gestures and feel that the correlation of feet (which walk) and hands (which carry: palms, flowers, song sheets, rosaries, candles) and voices (which sing and pray), that this harmonizing of three existential signs creates a very strong and supportive pattern of witnessing and praise.

Special Masses for children offer a great variety of opportunities for processions. Kindergarten or first grade students, for example, can join the liturgical ministers in the procession to the altar, accompanying the entrance hymn with the small rhythm instruments they have been using since September. (Psalm 150 would be especially appropriate!) This participation in the liturgy, "making a joyful noise to the Lord," will give the junior musicians a sense of belonging and the dignity of playing a role in what is taking place. The role is within their capacity and is of genuine service—not a gimmick. They might form an honor guard once more during the offertory procession and then return majestically to their classroom while the older children continue with the eucharistic celebration.

For celebrations of the Holy Spirit everyone can carry wind chimes they have made from swinging nails and pieces of tin or seashells or wood. The procession would of course be out of doors so the "wind of the spirit" may move freely through their chimes.

On another occasion a pair of eighth grade acolytes can meet each class at its schoolroom door and lead them, singing, to their places in the church. These acolytes could later join the offertory procession to the altar and remain in the sanctuary through the communion. On occasions when a class has prepared a special dance or pantomime, that class could join the entrance and departure processions with the other liturgical ministers.

Genuine processions ought to be restored as well to Masses where both children and adults are present. The meaning of the great ceremonies of the Easter Vigil, for example,

are seriously clouded when everyone remains seated, stretching necks backward to see the miniature gestures of the priests lighting a miniature fire in the vestibule. How much more truth does it communicate, and how much more deeply does it stir our hearts when we all gather around a caldron or bonfire in the churchyard, and then, carrying the new light, proceed to the place of scripture reading and then to the baptistry.

There was a time when Catholics rejoiced in many processions—processions to bless fields, processions around a house to bless each room, processions through the streets of the city with a feast day icon. We do not want to introduce or reintroduce customs that are inappropriate in our time. But surely the sense of involvement and ownership that ritual movement brings is important. Perhaps if we begin with the children, we will learn how to restore it to the adults as well. Have we not always thought of ourselves as a pilgrim church—a people on the move!

The Story Gift

— Elizabeth McMahon Jeep

Many years ago a group of us put together a program for vacation Bible school called "Coming to Our Senses." It was a catechesis on reconciliation, and as the name suggests it was designed around the theme of the prodigal son. Each morning for two weeks we began with a short prayer service for the whole group (grades one to eight) part of which was a reading of that parable. I am not sure how we arrived at the decision to repeat it each day, but I can remember worrying that we would bore the littlest ones to distraction. Looking back at that experience, however, I think we may have been right on the mark.

The story was used as our themesong, a motif for the work of each day and for the two weeks as a whole. We told other stories and sang songs and made posters and danced and dramatized and prayed and pondered, but always we came back to our anchor—our key image: "Once upon a time there was a man who had two sons. . . ." What I think we did by telling that story over and over again in a formal but comfortable setting—a prayerful setting—was enhance its stature, its mystery, and its significance for the children. We directed their ears and their hearts to it in much the same way that a yellow underliner directs the eye to a summarizing paragraph, or candles burning beside a painting announce that this is not like the other pictures in the room: it is an icon, to be studied and venerated and treasured because it carries a greater significance than the others.

What I think we did *wrong* during those lovely summer mornings, is spend too much time explaining the parable. We were so afraid that the children would not clearly understand that we drew diagrams and illustrations and explanations and implications and applications— and probably undercut the work our story was doing quite well enough on its own. We professional educators and religious people are so anxious to help children learn that we sometimes forget the distinction between image and idea, what can be experienced only and what can be explained.

The story of the prodigal son is an image, an icon. It does not explain God's mercy, it announces it. It cannot prove anything about God, it can only proclaim it in such a way that people of faith recognize its truth. It should not be explained, it is itself an explanation. We teachers were trying to help the children take the story into themselves by way of their rational sense, whereas it is only through the imagination that it can be rightly understood. What Mary Reed Newland has written concerning fairy tales is true of parables as well:

> One can exercise hope in the fairy tales and discover that in the end dragons are killed, and toads become princes who ride off with princesses to castles on mountains. Hope is the

great virtue of the fairy tales and we need to hope. We will die if we cannot. Children do not perceive all this but they need not; they need only have the stories. The seed is planted without their knowing that one day it will flower. ["The Magic of Storytelling," *Liturgy: Celebrating With Children*, The Liturgical Conference, 1981.]

We must be content to plant the seed, and not try to force it into bloom.

There was a time when I worried that we overdid the story of the prodigal son with young children. They do not, after all, turn their backs on God in the radical (we used to say "mortally sinful") way the story describes. There are other stories that are closer to the truth of their lives such as the gentle chiding Jesus gives the apostles who were quarreling over the best thrones in the kingdom—"me first! me first!" is a claim against the world that children of all ages are inclined to make.

But perhaps it is not so much the nature of the sin but the attitude of the father that shapes the story. In fact, the magnitude of the sin only serves to emphasize the security of our hope and our confidence in the warm welcome we will receive. And in a strange way the magnitude of festivity—the ring and the new clothes and the fatted calf—are only justified by the magnitude of the son's previous defection. Perhaps there is, hidden in the unconscious minds of the readers a recognition that the child *needs* to strike out on his own, to win his independence from the sheltering love of the father's house—even though he risks disaster. Otherwise he can never become an adult son. The elder brother in this story, we feel, does not have as profound a relationship with his father as does the younger son. He has maintained an element of subservience about his behavior—maybe that is why his relationship has never seemed to call for a celebration.

How deep the story can take us into the mystery of our relationship with God. How valuable a gift that Jesus has left with us to encourage us and strengthen us and call us back when we are wrong. How carefully and with what love we should hand it on to our children. It can be read to them, and told to them, and given to them in picture books and on cassettes. But most of all, we must proclaim the story and celebrate its truth in a liturgical way. Our rituals are filled with meaning beyond logic and are the most appropriate setting for the story that has something beyond logic to share with us.

Children, Music and the Mass

— Joyce Schemanske

Singing is of great importance in all celebrations, but it is to be especially encouraged in every way for Masses celebrated with children, in view of their special affinity for music. The culture of various groups and the capacities of the children present should be taken into account.

If possible the acclamations should be sung by the children rather than recited, especially the acclamations which are a part of the eucharistic prayer.
[*Directory for Masses with Children*, #30]

With these words the *Directory* points out an indisputable fact: music is integral to Masses with children, not something extra to be added or deleted at will. Children love to sing. Our challenge as teachers lies in choosing music that they are able to understand and that is relevant to their spiritual life, while providing a solid foundation for their eventual worship as adults.

Choosing Music for Children

Too often we underestimate our children's capabilities. We assume that the simplest music is best, offer the child a trite melody, a text of negligible quality and accompany them with three or four guitar chords. Few would argue that we must avoid trite music and concentrate on good music for our liturgies. ''Good'' music

---

JOYCE SCHEMANSKE is associate organist at Holy Name Cathedral, Chicago; her responsibilities include directing the grade school music program.

is often hard to define; however, there are criteria for judging a piece of music.

First and most important, all music used in the liturgy must be a vehicle for prayer, whether it is a newly composed guitar song, a traditional hymn or a Gregorian chant. Read a text first for its literary value; then ask whether it makes a sound theological statement. If a lyric does not stand up to these tests, it is not suitable for children no matter how catchy the melody may be.

''Good'' music for children is rhythmically interesting. Rhythmic music is not necessarily fast music, but any music based on a solid rhythmic pulse. Children also enjoy music that is syncopated: once the basic rhythmic pulse is established, they can easily sing ''off the beat.'' Dotted rhythms and music using repeated rhythmic patterns are also fit choices for children's songs provided that the rhythms are not repeated so often as to become monotonous.

A ''good'' melody usually contains a great deal of stepwise motion with a few strategically placed vocal leaps. Usually the leaps are followed by stepwise motion in the opposite direction of the leap. Melodies which primarily outline chords (triads) lack any sense of direction and quickly bore children. An example of a good melody is the hymn tune, *Lasst uns Erfreuen*, known with the texts ''All creatures of our God and King'' and ''Ye watchers and ye holy ones.'' This melody *also*

41

illustrates the use of repeated melodic patterns beginning on different steps of the scale (sequences). Training children to listen for these repeated patterns helps them to learn and remember melodies. As in the case of rhythmic patterns, melodic patterns must be interspersed with enough contrasting material to avoid becoming too repetitive.

Most of the characteristics of good music for children are also those of serious or classical music, especially that of Baroque composers such as J. S. Bach and G. F. Handel. Too often we overlook the possibilities of using classical music with children, assuming that it is too difficult and intellectual for them to comprehend. This is a mistake. Music does not appeal primarily to the intellect; it is felt by people intuitively—one reason music is called the universal language. Children are frequently more open to intuitive response than are adults. When children are exposed to serious music at an early age their appreciation for good music will develop.

Acquiring taste for music and literature can be compared. Although a child may derive momentary pleasure from reading comic books, there is little lasting value to be found in such reading. In the same way, we must avoid exposing our children only to music with superficial appeal and give them music of enduring worth. Liturgical music should challenge children to grow both musically and spiritually.

Fitting Music to the Mass

Concentrate on singing short acclamations rather than complete songs at first; children's Masses are one place where the "four-hymn syndrome" should be avoided at all costs. It is far better to sing only the gospel acclamation and the acclamations for the eucharistic prayer than to insert songs at the entrance, preparation of the gifts, communion and closing. The *Directory* points out the importance of the acclamations, particularly those of the eucharistic prayer. Children's experiences overflow into immediate, spontaneous responses, and the parts of the

liturgy which we sing should capitalize on this. To be an integral part of the child's worship experience, music must be connected with these most significant parts of the Mass.

The hymnal provides an excellent selection of material for music at the beginning or end of a celebration. Properly chosen hymns with good poetry expressing sound theology can inspire children spiritually and musically. When learning a hymn, have the children take turns reading the various verses and then putting into their own words what that verse is about. A hymn is musical poetry for prayer, and children are frequently quicker to intuit poetic symbolism than are adults.

A rich source for hymn melodies is authenic folk music: many hymnals include tunes that are drawn from English, Irish, Hebrew and American folk sources. Tunes such as *Slane* (Irish), *Shibbolet Basadeh* (Hebrew) and *Shaker Song* (American) are instant favorites with children. Folk songs are usually rhythmically predictable and often have pentatonic melodies (any melody which can be played using only the black notes on the piano) or modal melodies (i.e., "O come, O come, Emmanuel"), which are easier for children to sing and remember than are strictly diatonic melodies (i.e., "Holy, holy, holy," "Praise to the Lord"). The fact that folk melodies have been kept alive through oral tradition for centuries attests to their popularity.

One advantage that hymn tunes have over many contemporary guitar songs is that the rhythm and the melody stay the same for all the verses, unlike many songs which require minor changes in order to fit text to melody. There is a danger in assuming that guitar music is best for children, since the guitar cannot provide the strong melody reinforcement that children frequently need. When contemporary guitar music is suitable for children, it is best to add keyboard accompaniment to support the singing.

The liturgy of the word builds to the reading of the gospel, and the music we use should reflect this and grow in intensity. One way to achieve this is to sing the gospel acclamation in canon or round. Look through the many collections of canons and rounds which are available: "alleluia" is a frequently set text. An alleluia can be sung once by all in unison, then sung as a two- or three-part canon as the gospel procession continues. The acclamation can be tailored to the actual length of the procession and end on a signal from the director. Because they have only one word to remember, the children will be able to watch the procession while they sing. Children love the challenge of singing in parts; the use of rounds and canons allows them to do this and at the same time provides musical elaboration at an appropriate moment in the liturgy.

The eucharistic prayers for children particularly lend themselves to musical participation. The acclamations are short and easily memorized ("Hosanna in the highest," "Jesus has given his life for us," etc.). The use of short, tuneful acclamations is an excellent way to draw the children into the important action of the eucharistic prayer. (See "The Eucharistic Prayers for Children" for a fuller discussion.)

If an adult is able to serve as cantor, many options are open to you. The psalm may be sung with the cantor singing the verses and the children the refrain. In similar fashion, the Lamb of God may be sung with cantor singing the petitions and children responding, "have mercy on us." Music at communion is also best handled by a cantor singing verses and the children answering with a simple, memorized antiphon: it is asking too much of a child to carry a song sheet or hymnal and take communion at the same time.

At many liturgies a cantor is not available. But possibilities abound for music at communion, as well as for music during the preparation of the gifts. One class could learn a special song to sing at that time and then take communion while the others are returning to their seats. If there is a school choir, this is an excellent chance for them to sing. A few children in any group take private music lessons: flute, clarinet, violin, etc. Ask these children to bring in pieces that they are working on and see if they would be suitable for church use. If the piece does not have a written accompaniment, the organist or guitarist can work one out. Consider using several instrumentalists. Select a canon and have each child learn it, then perform it as an ensemble piece. Because the harmonic structures are usually fairly simple, use a student guitarist as the accompanist. In addition many schools have Orff and other rhythm instruments available which can be used in a variety of ways in the acclamations and hymns. The only limit is the creativity of the music director.

These are a few of the possibilities for liturgical music with children. Each group of children brings to the liturgy differing abilities, resources and levels of spiritual development. By consistently using good music creatively to challenge our children's musical and spiritual growth, we will enable them to become fully participating members of the worshiping community.

Children and Ministries

— Elizabeth McMahon Jeep

At a signal the first grade students quietly took off their shoes. They filed out of their pews, walked in procession to the sanctuary, circled the altar and waited. Then the music began and, as the congregation sang the Our Father, the young people moved into a very simple but lovely gesture-dance. When it was over they returned to their seats and put their shoes back on—with smiles a mile wide and a sense of accomplishment that was almost tangible. The liturgical dance was very successful—it was smoothly accomplished; it enlivened the liturgy without interrupting its pace; it was simple without being cute; it drew the attention of the other children to the Our Father and not to the performance of the first graders. The dancers, then, were serving as liturgical ministers, focusing and encouraging the prayer of the congregation.

Such events are common at school Masses. For the past 20 years teachers and pastors have racked their brains to come up with ways to involve school age children more actively in what is going on. While liturgists and teachers do not always agree on what will enhance the prayer of student congregations and what might interrupt or even detract from it (heaven knows we have all seen what looked like liturgical circus acts!) there seems to be agreement on three points. We have learned a lot in the past 20 years! We are still a long way from clear "solutions" to the children's worship "problem." Progress will come through sensitive experimentation and thoughtful evaluation.

One aspect of children's liturgy that needs more attention is the area of ministerial roles—not just "make-work" jobs that give children a feeling of participation, but the essential ministries upon which the prayer of the community depends.

There are four types of ministry that children can exercise, depending upon their age and the adult guidance they receive.

Preparation. There is no recognized church order of liturgy planners and no official commissioning necessary, so nothing prevents children from taking a place on the committee that selects hymns, or prepares visual materials to enhance the environment of worship, or sets out the vestments and gifts. These duties seldom call for specialized talents and are generally offered to students on a rotating basis. By the time children reach junior high, they should have developed a sense of the variety of ministries available, the relationship between preparing carefully and worshiping well, an appreciation of the service behind-the-scenes work provides for the community, and the ability to teach younger children some of the skills they have learned. Children usually love these jobs and with the slightest encouragement will approach them with reverence and creativity. It is salutary to expect the same committees to prepare the liturgy and to straighten up after it is over. This helps them see the process through to completion and avoids the paternalistic overtones that develop wherever adults do all the clean-up chores.

Hospitality. This is the responsibility of those whom the community calls to be ushers. Students from about third grade on are increasingly capable of helping participants find seats, greeting guests, seeing that everyone has copies of the music, making sure the gift bearers are in order before the offertory procession begins, and indicating to the younger children when to move forward for communion. It is the ushers' responsibility to facilitate the comfort, movement and participation of the congregation. The development of this ministry will eliminate much of the traffic duty and other bustling around that teachers sometimes do during a children's Mass.

Altar servers. Just as the ushers serve the congregation, the acolytes serve the comfort, movement and participation of the presider and other ministers such as the lector or minister of communion. This role of assistant is an important function in the Catholic liturgy, which is rich in gesture, movement, symbols and sensible objects. The presider should have his hands free and should not leave the altar to fetch something, move a candle, put away a paten. Servers need to study and practice so that they understand the flow of the ceremony and can interpret a nod or look from the presider. More than any other student minister, these children need to be able to handle themselves and objects with reverence and dignity, so that they can move about when needed without calling attention to themselves.

Specialized roles. Depending on the liturgy, some children may serve as lectors, commentators, petitioners, musicians (players of the recorder or flute, operators of the phonograph or tape deck), singers, dancers, mimes. Children must be able to see these services as an offering for the good of the praying community, and not as opportunities for showing off. They also need enough training to be secure in their task. With lectors especially, it is essential that they have a chance to practice their readings in the assembly area that will be used, with a microphone if one will be needed. As a general rule, children of any age can be asked to read in their own classroom celebrations; children fourth grade and older may be asked to read at a school liturgy, but a child younger than seventh or eighth grade should not ordinarily be asked to read at a family Mass where a substantial number of adults are present.

Helpful books are available for the teaching of servers, but common sense will have to guide the preparation of students for other roles, especially roles at noneucharistic liturgies. Exercises can be designed to develop poise in walking, sitting, standing, carrying a book, moving a pitcher, lighting a candle. This will help children develop a sense of dignity and will perhaps encourage some who might not do so otherwise to volunteer for ministerial roles. In general all they need to remember is: read slowly, walk slowly, hold things high, control your nervousness (even priests are sometimes nervous, expect it, don't worry about it), keep from squirming, keep your mind on who you are and what you are doing—your action is prayer, your action is helping others to pray.

This is, after all, what ministry is all about—serving the servants of God.

Putting the Pieces Together

— Robert W. Hovda

Attention to the experience of the participants is not a new consideration in liturgical celebration. As a matter of fact, it is as old as any theological reflection about common prayer. God invites our worship not for God's benefit but for our own. Because only when we focus on God's love and care, forgiveness and grace, do we get ourselves together and find our place.

Attention to the experience of the participants is not new, despite the lack of it in the period of liturgical decadence from which we are now emerging. Some decades ago in *Orate Fratres* (now *Worship*), the late Gerald Vann commented on the statement of a famous European Catholic that "the idea of conducting services primarily for the edification of the faithful smacks of Protestantism." Vann wrote: "Alas for St. Thomas. Alas for St. Paul's great guiding 'rubric' in 1 Corinthians 14:26. Alas for every theologian who has written on prayer, from Origen and St. Cyprian to St. Thomas and Suarez, who has been at pains to explain that we 'address God' not to 'edify' him, but precisely to 'edify' ourselves."

A modern recovery of the gospel's personalist emphasis has enabled us again in our time to attend to the experience of the

ROBERT W. HOVDA, a priest of the diocese of Fargo, North Dakota, has written and lectured widely on liturgical topics.

participants in worship, whether they are children or adults or both. Attention to their experience has brought us along far beyond our "vernacular-time" fascination with words and texts—to a renewed appreciation of the multileveled and multidimensional communication of good liturgy, involving the sensual and sensible as well as the rational, the body as well as the mind, the emotions and feelings as well as the intellect.

Rites Need Rhythm

When experience, rather than merely instruction, is asserted again as a primary test of good common prayer, then the sustained involvement of all participants comes to be seen clearly as a requirement. Anything but sustained involvement—e.g., boredom, distraction, daydreaming—is the enemy of good experience. Such a sustained involvement in turn requires variety, rhythm, alternation in the structure or format or progression of any service of public worship. While adults can sustain attention for longer periods and can deal with more abstract language, the principle holds for all age groups with undiminished force.

All of us need the variety and alternation we find in the traditional structures of liturgical rites. It is apparent in the hours, the eucharist, the other sacraments. In each of the traditional structures, we can discern and feel a certain rhythm: not only a beginning, a middle and an end, but also alternation among persons and groups of persons, among groupings of elements into a preparation and a building up and a climax and a descent, between sound and silence, between movement and stillness, between song and speech, between the familiar and the spontaneous, between proclamation and reflection, between word and deed.

The difference between children's liturgies and adult liturgies is not in these various and necessary alternations, which any group of human beings requires in order to sustain involvement and participation. One difference, however, will certainly be that the elements to be alternated in children's liturgies *must be* more brief and more concrete than the various parts of a liturgy with adults. Critical requirements for children, this brevity and concreteness of each element or part of a rite are frequently advantageous for adults as well. So we need not feel that we are depriving the latter group of spiritual sustenance when we take those requirements into account in our planning.

Of Processions and Punctuation

Some examples may help clarify what we have called "rhythm" or alternation in liturgical structures. A reading is never followed by another reading. It may be followed by reflective song, or reflective silence, or on special occasions a mime or dance reflection on it. But the proclamation of a reading has to stand out as something integral, something worth reflecting about. Responsory psalms or songs, therefore, are to be sung, not read. If they cannot be sung, they are better omitted in favor of silence.

Any processional movement, whether of ministers or of congregation as a whole, is aided by song, or at least by instrumental music. In the eucharist, this is true above all of the most important procession, the climactic procession for the sharing of holy communion. The activity of the communion procession and sharing and song, for the sake of a good rhythm or alternation, yields to what? To more

song? Would it not be more appropriate to see that it yields to stillness and silence?

A service of public worship, like any other public assembly, requires punctuation and definition. Minimally, for example, the punctuation of a specific greeting by the presider at the beginning and a clear dismissal at the end is indispensable for a feeling of shape and form. Beyond that, ritual action demands and deserves the kind of orchestration or choreography that builds gradually, smoothly, steadily toward a climax, and then, rather swiftly and gently, moves to dismissal.

All of this is common sense as well as liturgical tradition and law. Unfortunately, it takes a special effort to apply common sense to habitual actions. Ritual celebration because of its habitual character tends to escape the scrutiny of common sense. Planners, therefore, need to look very carefully not only at the individual elements, the various parts, of any celebration, but also at the sequence of the elements or parts, their relation to one another and to the entire action.

Vocal prayers must not be piled upon vocal prayers, nor song upon song, nor gesture upon gesture. If any of these is worth doing, it deserves definition, integrity, uncluttered articulation. Each deserves to be taken seriously enough to be permitted to stand on its own feet, to accomplish its particular purpose, and to help us move on in a progressive and coherent fashion.

No Place for Fillers

In other words, we have no fillers in a well-planned liturgical action. No part or element is introduced simply because we have to pass the time. We do not "throw in" a song because someone likes it, or interpose a gesture because it is familiar, or include a dance because we have a dancer. If someone likes a song, if a gesture is familiar, if local talent is available, that is certainly a plus. But anything that is to be part of a liturgy must pass the tests of quality and appropriateness.

No art form, for example, is in and of itself alien to or unacceptable in liturgical celebration. This is just as true of dance and mime and drama and film or slide projection as it is of music and painting and sculpture and stained glass. The question is not, Which arts are acceptable? The proper questions regard the quality of art and its appropriate use.

Quality is no less important for children's celebrations than it is for adult or general ones. Perhaps it is even more important when dealing with children, because children are open and in the process of formation. Children still have a chance of achieving a greater appreciation of beauty, authenticity, craftsmanship, skill, color and shape, texture, etc. Most adults are profoundly affected by our culture's general insensitivity and even blindness with regard to quality.

Applied to human talents employed in celebration (e.g., readers, song leaders, singers, instrumentalists, acolytes, hosts or ushers, dancers, actors, presiders), quality has reference to training, competence, skill, practice. Applied to objects employed either as part of the environment of celebration or within the celebrative action (e.g., building interior, seating, decoration, altar, candles, cross, vessels, vesture, book), quality involves craftsmanship, art, honesty and genuineness, simplicity, beauty of form and color, the personal stamp of an artist, and similar considerations. If many of us adults have been deprived of this kind of sensitivity, we owe our children an opportunity—by every means possible, including liturgical celebration—for a broader and richer development of their human faculties.

All that can be said, however, about quality environment, quality performance, quality symbols and art and visuals is not enough. Liturgy makes even greater demands than that. For liturgy, as we have indicated, is a community action with definition and orchestration. Every element, every part, must be appropriate. Appropriateness is a criterion that must be applied as rigorously as quality. With reference to art objects, we have to ask: Is it an integral and harmonious part of an environment suitable for celebration? Or is it simply clutter and irrelevance?

With reference to talents or ministries or elements we might consider for a particular service of worship, appropriateness can be judged by similar questions: Does it support and enhance the action of the rite? Or is it a kind of interruption or intermission in the normal progress of the particular liturgy? If we can answer yes to the former, we can embrace and employ any art and any element. If the answer to the latter question is yes, then no matter how good the quality, it cannot claim a place in liturgy.

IV. Understanding the Mass

An Overview of the Mass

— Gabe Huck

Sometimes it helps to step back. Even someone who has been at Mass every Sunday since a child, someone who has been involved in planning liturgies with children for years, needs to stand back occasionally and ponder the eucharistic liturgy. Distance can refresh.

Such pondering could spring from a dozen different motives, could take as guide the scriptures, the fathers of the church, poets, preachers, theologians. There are insights of many kinds in the lives and writings of this Catholic people that through 100 generations and all the lands of the earth have gathered to listen to their scriptures and to bless the bread and wine.

For those who are responsible in some way for the manner in which children and adults celebrate the Mass, however, these occasional reflections might often be on the structure of the liturgy itself. This can be helpful, practical, yes, but can also refresh and remind. What follows is such a very basic look at the ritual we Catholics call the Mass.

This is offered not because such knowledge is essential. Children, adults and old people pray the Mass enthusiastically and devoutly without ever learning the names or histories of its various rites. But for·those charged with planning for good liturgy, those who would

GABE HUCK is director of Liturgy Training Publications of the archdiocese of Chicago. His books include *Liturgy with Style and Grace* and *A Book of Family Prayer*.

explain our rites to children, a good knowledge of the rite is vital.

Gathering Around Book and Table

Sometimes liturgy seems like a lot of little items that simply need to be arranged in the proper order. Sign of the cross before greeting. Greeting before penitential rite. Penitential rite before Gloria or prayer. Even when planners arrange and rearrange, the Mass can still feel like a number of isolated activities. That's not liturgy.

The strange thing is that this outlook has much in common with one that at first seems quite different. Some understand the Mass as a series of "therefores." "We have made the sign of the cross. Therefore, I greet you." "We have prayed our Creed. Therefore, let us join in the prayer of the faithful." They seem to think the Mass was put together by a logician!

A realistic view is quite different. We Christians, like any tribe, have evolved some very beautiful and really quite simple ways to gather together and express in symbols what we as a people are about, what we mean, what we believe. For us at Mass, those symbols are the speaking of and listening to the scriptures, and the gathering at the holy table to bless bread and wine and to share the body and blood of Christ. The different ages and cultures have done this with ease and in ways that seemed good and beautiful to them, and have handed the tradition on. We do the same and invite our children to learn to do this Christian ritual.

These two central deeds—the sharing of scripture, and the blessing and sharing of food—are not unique to our tribe. We find them among many peoples. Any family, any town, any society that has a strong sense of itself has times when people gather to repeat the stories. In the family this may come on Thankgiving Day or at a family reunion; it may come when there is a wedding or a funeral. Whether gathered at a picnic table or a casket, when people feel there is something to belong to they have their stories to tell and retell.

In the same way, elements of ritual cling to our meals when we gather on special occasions or with persons dear to us. This may find expression in a prayer, a toast, the preparation of traditional foods, the special setting of the table, the willingness to have peace and good conversation among all.

The first Christians were Jews who were raised with both kinds of rituals. Their weekly Sabbath liturgy was built around the gradual reading of their story as found in the Torah (first five books of the Bible) with portions from the prophets. The great holy days of the year were marked by ritual meals (the paschal lamb, for example), and each week's Sabbath had its festive setting of the table and prayers. In fact, every meal began with a prayer of blessing and thanksgiving. This was how Jesus learned to pray. These were the ways his followers prayed, but their prayers were filled also with Jesus and with the life he had shared with them.

The first generations of Christians gathered on the first day of each week for a table ritual—to "break bread" as they called it. Bread and wine were brought by the people, over them the presider led the people in prayer of praise and thanksgiving for all God had done, especially in his servant Jesus. Then the bread would be broken and shared, the wine drunk. Pieces of the holy bread would be taken home to the sick and others who could not attend, thus extending the holy communion.

Almost always the prayer that was spoken over the bread and wine recalled how Jesus had taken bread and said: "This is my body." And he had taken the cup: "This is the cup of my blood." They prayed that the Holy Spirit would come upon these gifts.

Our liturgy of the eucharist is very little changed from this. We still place these same simple foods on the table, give thanks to the Father, remember the words of Jesus and call upon the Spirit. We still break the bread and share it. We still drink from the cup. Our Christian ancestors also continued to read the Torah together, sometimes in the synagogues and sometimes in their own gatherings. Very often they did this before the breaking of the bread. To the readings from the Hebrew Scriptures they came to add the writings of the apostles and the gospels. Eventually, the two rituals—this orderly reading of the sacred scriptures and the breaking of the bread—were always done together.

Through the centuries, the elaborations of these two rites took on a variety of forms. Different theologies, often in reaction to one false teaching or another, had their impact. (For example, when some denied that Christ was truly God, the church reacted with stronger affirmations of his divinity. In the liturgy this led to feelings of unworthiness and infrequent communion.) We are now in a period when we have some insight into the origins and meaning of our liturgy, but have only begun to learn to make these rites of scripture and eucharist devout and sincere expressions of our Christian lives.

The liturgy of the word and the liturgy of the eucharist do not begin and end abruptly. Human beings naturally find ways to lead into important moments. So at Mass, we have several brief rituals that form the "introductory rites" and, before the eucharist itself begins, we have a time called "preparation of the altar and gifts." Both are times not only for physical preparation— getting people and things in their place—but also for allowing our minds and spirits to pass from one activity to another. Likewise, the conclusion is a number of short rites that take us from the time of prayer and community back to our individual lives and work.

The Introductory Rites

From entering the room where the liturgy will be done until the reader begins the first reading: this is the introduction to prayer. Some of it is informal, some formal. The purpose (see DMC #40) is twofold: to give people the sense of doing the Mass together, and to establish a mood in which they can really hear the scriptures and celebrate the eucharist. We have traditional ways of doing that. Singing together is one of them. When we sing we hear each other, we lose our voice in the voices of many. This gives a good sense of community. The song that is used may also set a mood that says we are in Lent or in Eastertime. We use other ways of entering prayer together—the sign of the cross (the basic Christian gesture, here made all together), the greeting, some form of reflective penitential rite, the Gloria, the invitation to prayer and the opening prayer.

In Masses with children, only one or two elements will be used. Often the children are from classes, each will know some others well. There will be likes and dislikes, feelings of superiority and inferiority. Introductory rites cannot be expected to make all this into a model of community. They should rather show simply what community there is—the community of the cross, the community perhaps that the song expresses. The presider's leadership, especially in the invitation, "Let us pray," and in the silence which follows, is quite important. The leadership of presider and of other ministers (song leader, for example) must keep the ritual from becoming idle repetition. *This* sign of the cross, *this* singing a song, *this* keeping of prayerful silence must express their own full presence to the children.

The introductory rites are not to be elaborate. During Advent/Christmastime or Lent/Eastertime they will be shaped by the season. They create a space to enter into prayer together. They are not necessarily that prayer themselves. A simple format in the hands of competent leaders will serve well. Complication, in any hands, usually will not.

The Liturgy of the Word

We have noted that this is a storytelling ritual. It is more than this, of course, for the stories are about us, about who we mean to be. They come from our sacred scriptures and take the shape of letters, poems, visions, parables, narratives, histories. At Sunday Mass, three selections are read, the last being always from the gospels. With children, it is usually best to use only one or two readings, sometimes shortening them. The gospel selection is always to be read. The reading selected should, when possible, be in keeping with the season; the language should not be made childish. During Ordinary Time, readings are assigned to each weekday or feast day. When these are not appropriate, consider the readings of the Sunday just past or approaching. If the children are hearing the scriptures regularly in the home and classroom, they will be acquiring gradually the ability to listen to these isolated segments within the larger context. Introductory comments, brief and carefully thought out, may help in preparing the children to hear the day's scripture.

The reading itself must be done as well as possible. Although the children should serve in the various ministerial roles when they can do this well, it should not be presumed that a child must do the readings. Ordinarily stories are told *to* children *by* adults. The child is not neglected when the role expected is listening. Listening is something active (which children can teach us).

The liturgy of the word, even with a reduced number of readings, should provide some silent time for reflection on the scripture or the homily, and the opportunity to sing. A psalm may be used between two readings, perhaps a psalm the children will be hearing on the Sundays of the season and can now learn, or perhaps the same psalm used through many seasons so that the children can make it a part of their own prayer (with classroom discussion and suggestions: is it a good night prayer? meal prayer?).

The homily, given by someone gifted in speaking with children, may or may not take the form of a dialogue, but it must do what a good homily always does: unfold the scriptures so that they are seen to be our story.

The liturgy of the word concludes with the prayers of the faithful, the general intercessions. These should be felt as the prayer of the church: for itself, for those in authority, for the poor and suffering, for the local community. Intercession is the task of the Christian, but it must be seen in its full sweep, not just in the immediate and personal sense. The sung litany, even with children, may be the best ordinary form of this prayer; even this form can leave places for the children to speak their own words. Planners should realize, though, that the words are not so crucial: what matters is giving ourselves to the work of intercession, of holding up the needs of the whole world before the Lord, and that takes a strong ritual form such as the chant with the refrain ''Lord, have mercy'' or ''Lord, hear our prayer'' repeated over and over.

The Preparation of Altar and Gifts

This is another time of transition. It is a brief and quiet time between the more community-centered moments. But it is not to be sloppy. The main focus is the setting of the table in which only a few persons normally participate. Others may be seated and quiet. Some music may be played. Those who bring forward the cloth, book, cup, wine, plate and bread do so with reverence: not with the ''foreignness'' of doing something unfamiliar in public, but with a comfortable sense of doing something special on behalf of others. The presider should not do things for the children but take only his part when the table is prepared. This is ordinarily not the time to bring forward other gifts. They can be carried in the entrance procession.

The Liturgy of the Eucharist

The eucharistic prayers for Masses with children, especially the second of these, give a clear picture of the kind of prayer this is. It is not the monologue of the presider, stopping now and then for a little song from the assembly. Rather, it is a great prayer of praise and thanksgiving spoken by the presider on behalf of all those present who join in many times with the sung acclamations. In this is its strength: the gathering around a table on which rest only the book, the bread and the wine; the sincere address to the Father of our thanksgiving, alternating between the words of the presider and the acclamations of the assembly. If all of us, children and adults, are learning to give thanks to God through every day, then we will want this summation of all that living and thanksgiving. It is not to seem the longest moment in the liturgy; in its sense of active participation it should seem the strongest. The use of gesture with the singing of acclamation can assist this if it becomes as natural as genuflection or making the sign of the cross.

The moments which follow flow from the eucharistic prayer and speak of who we are: the holy communion. The Lord's Prayer, the peace greeting, the breaking of the bread and Lamb of God, the communion itself. These are simple rites not to be rushed. The Lord's Prayer can be spoken or sung. Unless a local community has a gesture of unity that is more natural to the child's world than a handshake, the peace greeting may often be omitted. The breaking of the bread depends for its importance on the presider's breaking the one loaf into many pieces while all watch and join in the litany, Lamb of God. Communion itself should be done with great reverence and a sense for the holiness of the moment—holiness that we find in ourselves as the church and in the bread and wine that are Christ's body and blood. The singing of a simple refrain, known by heart, children alternating with cantor, might accompany or follow the communion. But silence is also important after communion and before the prayer which concludes the liturgy of the eucharist.

Concluding Rites

Again, the ritual allows for a transition, this time from prayer and community to our individual lives. There is a blessing, which can be made stronger with the longer blessings and the often repeated "amen," and the dismissal. The latter may include some special words appropriate to this particular gathering.

A final caution: as noted in the *Directory for Masses with Children* (#24), adults who are present for the liturgy should be present as participants, present to pray and not to watch, not to monitor, not to discipline. A very great deal depends on this.

The Eucharistic Prayers for Children

— Robert H. Oldershaw

> The eucharistic prayer is of the greatest importance in the eucharist celebrated with children because it is the high point of the entire celebration. Much depends upon the manner in which the priest proclaims this prayer and in which the children take part by listening and making their acclamations.
> [*Directory for Masses with Children* #52]

This short statement makes three critical points. (1) The eucharistic prayer is of the greatest importance because it is the high point of the entire celebration. (2) The way the presider proclaims the prayer is all important. (3) The prayer can be the high point of the celebration only if the children are drawn into it through both their listening and acclaiming.

The Eucharistic Prayer

Several years ago Ralph Keifer writing in *Worship* said: "The eucharistic prayer can only succeed as the central prayer of the church when it is treated as such. . . . The eucharistic prayer must actually appear, as celebrated, as the paradigm of the common prayer of the church, of all and for all. . . . If music is to have a place in the liturgy, it should be here that our people sing, *if nowhere else*." Keifer notes that the people's acclamations "are not handy frills to keep them awake and 'following

Father's prayer.' They are ways of having the people enter verbally into the act of offering at the points which are most important." ("The Noise in Our Solemn Assemblies," *Worship*, January, 1971)

This holds true for children as well as adults. Within a year of the publication of the *Directory for Masses with Children* three new eucharistic prayers for use with children had been approved by the Holy See. One of the significant features of the new eucharistic prayers was the introduction of additional acclamations within the body of the prayer.

Even with the acclamations, however, the challenge to draw the children from the periphery of the celebration into the very heart of the liturgy is still considerable. It is all too current practice to tack music onto the edges of the eucharist (e.g., a hymn at beginning, offertory, communion and the end) rather than beginning at the center with the acclamations of the eucharistic prayer and working outwards. As Keifer says: "The real question is not whether the acclamations in the eucharistic prayer should be sung, but whether the eucharistic prayer can appear as significant when they are not. It is impossible to be attentive to such a lengthy narrative unless it is vigorously punctuated with song." The eucharistic prayers for children with many more acclamations provide a marvelous opportunity to engage children in the most basic and central part of the eucharistic service.

ROBERT H. OLDERSHAW, a priest of the archdiocese of Chicago, serves as associate director for music of the Chicago Office for Divine Worship.

The Presider's Role

Much of this depends on the presider. "He is in a unique position to *lead* the assembly in prayer by his presence and style. Even his speech patterns can help provide a verbal environment in which the children will feel drawn into the prayer. His manner, therefore, will be of great assistance in helping the children know when to come in with the acclamations." (*BCL Report*, no. 1)

What the Bishops' Committee on the Liturgy suggests has actually happened in this writer's experience. His pastor, through care and attentiveness, has evoked a wonderful response from children using the Peloquin setting of Eucharistic Prayer for Children II. This does not so much require musical skill as a great deal of caring and rehearsing. Good celebrations, as spontaneous as they may appear, do not happen by accident—they are well rehearsed and well planned.

Drawing Children into the Prayer

The eucharistic prayer will be central to the celebration when the children enter into it through acclamations which are full, exuberant and bright, and which vigorously punctuate the prayer. In their 1980 report, the BCL said: "To presume that singing these acclamations is too difficult for children is to deprive them of a fuller participation in liturgical and communal prayer. Children readily respond to active participation when properly led to understand their role and to invest their time and energies in it."

There are currently a number of musical settings which enable children to participate fully in the eucharistic prayer and to experience it as the high point of the entire celebration.

Both Father Ralph Verdi, CPPS, and Sister Theophane Hytrek, OSF, have composed settings for all three prayers. They are published in the *BCL Report*, no. 1. An accompaniment for keyboard and/or guitar is available, though the music may be sung a cappella. The Verdi setting also makes provision for clapping and/or rhythm instruments. Both composers have written attractive, rhythmic melodies.

Verdi has said that music for the eucharistic prayer attempts to reinforce and enhance the text and make it easy for the people to respond through a synchronization of presider's and people's parts. Music effects a bond between presider and assembly from the introductory dialogue to the amen. These settings would profit from the presence of a music minister who, with a brief introduction on keyboard or guitar, can indicate entrances, rhythm and melodic pattern.

In the setting "Eucharistic Prayer II for Masses with Children" by Richard Proulx (GIA Publications) the presider sings some parts and recites others. Proulx produces melodic sequences which thread their way through the entire prayer, thus producing cumulative, climactic effects. Moreover, the melodic sequences in the beginning of the prayer serve as built-in rehearsals for all that follows. A variety of shorter acclamations meld into the Sanctus and return again at the end to form an amen in canon. The children themselves play the instruments (as many as desired): xylophone, glockenspiel, handbells, fingercymbals, tabor, triangle, tambourine, Chinese bells, timpani and organ. The instrumentation is used in Orff-like patterns, easily remembered and piled one on top of the other like building blocks. The melodies are simple and childlike, utilizing the best part of the child's vocal range. The composer capitalizes on the remarkable memory logic and innate musicality of children.

Alexander Peloquin in the eucharistic prayer from "Unless You Become: A Liturgy for Children" (GIA Publications) provides "a lively and rhythmic song involving the presider, two choirs and congregation." Instruments include flute, trumpets, trombones, drum, string bass, tambourine and triangle. Spontaneity and joy are the qualities; bright orchestral colors and transparency of sound are the elements of the tonal fabric. The hosannas, which incorporate gesture as well as song, are set to a chime or bell motif in backward version. They punctuate the prayer and become more spontaneous, brilliant and exciting as the prayer unfolds. In Peloquin's setting, the hosanna is the only acclamation sung throughout. It can be sung a cappella and can be taught to a group of children in a matter of minutes. In this writer's experience with school liturgies, the use of this eucharistic prayer setting with its easily learned hosanna has been more effective than many words in teaching the children the centrality of the eucharistic prayer. If the musical focal point of the Mass is the eucharistic prayer—if less music is sung on the edges and more in the center—the medium itself becomes the message.

Other musical settings are available (for example, one by Carey Landry arranged for guitar/keyboard, presider and children from his collection *Bloom Where You're Planted*, published by North American Liturgy Resources).

The eucharistic prayers for Masses with children use clear and poetic language. Combined with the available musical settings, they present a unique opportunity to draw the children into the heart of the eucharistic celebration "so that the offering of the church becomes their offering with Christ to the eternal Father in the Holy Spirit." (DMC #52)

Planning Chart for Masses with Children

— Elizabeth McMahon Jeep

The chart on the following pages outlines the Order of Mass as it most often occurs on a Sunday in Ordinary Time and as it *might* occur with an assembly of children according to the requirements of the *Directory for Masses with Children*. A comparison of the two outlines ("Ritual elements" and "Elements of Masses with children") reveals the latitude which the *Directory* provides for celebrations with children. It is equally apparent that planners and presiders must exercise considerable judgment when planning celebrations of Mass with children: the *Directory* outlines only the "principal rites and prayers" which are always to be included.

A look at the "Ritual elements" and "Children's action" columns makes it clear that at the usual Sunday celebration children are seldom physically involved in the ritual of the Mass. While, for example, some children may take part in the procession with the gifts, most will not leave their seats. Children participate at Sunday Mass primarily by listening and making verbal or sung responses.

The *Directory* insists, however, that "every effort should be made to increase [children's] participation and to make it more intense." (#22) By means of the preparations, the place of celebration, song, gesture, posture, procession, pictures, liturgical ornament, color, text, silent reflection and the manner of the ministers, says the *Directory,* "the liturgy is never to appear as something dry and merely intellectual." (#25) While the required elements for Masses with children may seem spare, especially in comparison with the complexity of Mass celebrated with adults, the *Directory*'s suggestions and guidelines provide for ample, rich celebrations. (See "DMC references.")

The first rule of planning Masses with children is not to add layer upon layer of new activity, but to do the essential things well in ways that engage children. The chart includes "Spirit of the action" and "Considerations for planners" to assist this. The planner's principal job is to understand the meaning and action of the Mass, and to clarify it so that children are able to pray it.

Introductory Rites

Purpose
To unify the congregation; to establish an atmosphere of common prayer.

Ritual Elements*	Children's Action	Spirit of the Action	Elements of Masses with Children†	DMC References
ENTRANCE SONG/Procession	Sing	The ministers (or the entire community) "go to the altar of God" in procession. An opening song unites the congregation in prayer.	One *introductory element*	#40 introductory elements
				#34 entrance procession
SIGN OF THE CROSS/AMEN	Gesture/Respond	All Christian worship is done in the name of the Father, Son and Holy Spirit.		
Greeting/RESPONSE (there are several alternatives)	Respond	The presider may introduce the focus for the day's prayer after the greeting.		
I CONFESS . . . (or alternative penitential rite or blessing and sprinkling holy water)	Speak	The community seeks reconciliation with one another and God before bringing its sacrifice to the altar.		#23 language of penitential rite
LORD, HAVE MERCY	Respond (Sing)	This acclamation praises the Lord and asks for his love.		
May almighty God . . ./AMEN	Respond			
GLORIA	Speak (Sing)	An ancient Christian hymn of praise and thanksgiving.		#31 musical settings of Gloria

Opening prayer SILENT PRAYER/AMEN	Listen/Respond	A "collect," or gathering prayer, which expresses the focus of the celebration. The presider gathers our needs and addresses them to the Father in Jesus' name.	*Opening prayer*	#40 importance of opening prayer
				#37 manner of speaking prayers
				#50 selection of prayer
				#51 adaptation of prayer

* elements in CAPITAL LETTERS indicate participation by children

† required elements *italicized;* suggested elements enclosed in parentheses

Considerations for Planners

Prepare the environment so that it contributes to establishing the spirit of the celebration. The place for worship should be one in which "the children can conduct themselves freely according to the demands of a living liturgy that is suited to their age." (#25)

Provide a gracious and dynamic beginning. "Avoid any excess of rites in this part of Mass" (#40) by highlighting one or more elements and suppressing others. Do not omit the same elements all the time.

- How shall we actively engage the children from the very beginning of the liturgy? (Song, procession, environment, meditative or mood music, greeting, commentary?)
- Shall we use a penitential or baptismal element? Why? (Song, commentary, sign of peace, dance, visual?)
- Shall we use the Gloria? (Sung? Shortened?)
- What shall the opening prayer be?

KEY

Ritual Elements outlines the order of Mass for *an ordinary Sunday.* Elements printed in CAPITAL LETTERS indicate participation by children.

Children's Action indicates the manner of participation at Mass on *an ordinary Sunday.*

Spirit of the Action is a commentary on the elements of the Mass.

Elements of Masses with Children outlines the ritual elements which are always to be included in a Mass with children; these required elements are *italicized.* Possible additions to the Mass which the *Directory* suggests for the benefit of children are enclosed in parentheses.

DMC References lists the paragraphs of the *Directory for Masses with Children* which comment on particular parts of the Mass.

Liturgy of the Word

Purpose
To remember God's saving deeds so that our praise and thanksgiving is genuine; to be reminded of his call so that we can recommit ourselves as God's people.

Ritual Elements*	Children's Action	Spirit of the Action	Elements of Masses with Children†	DMC References
	Listen/Sit		(Introduction which puts feast or scriptures in context.)	#47 introductory comments
First reading	Listen	A proclamation from the Hebrew Scriptures or Acts of the Apostles.		#29 preparation for readings of the liturgy #41 use of scripture #42 number of readings #43 selection, source and editing of readings #44 criterion for selecting readings
This is the word . . ./ THANKS BE TO GOD	Respond			
Responsorial psalm/ REFRAIN	Sing	A psalm which reflects the spirit of the reading is sung.	(Reflective silence may substitute for responsorial psalm.)	#46 use of psalm, alleluia, silence #37 use of silence
Second reading	Listen	A proclamation from a New Testament writing—usually theological rather than narrative, and too abstract for children.		
Gospel acclamation/ ALLELUIA (or alternative)	Sing/Stand	We welcome the gospel joyfully by singing an alleluia or other acclamation.		#34 procession with gospel book
The Lord be with you/ AND ALSO WITH YOU	Respond			
Gospel reading	Listen	A proclamation from one of the gospels.	Gospel reading	#42 use of gospel
A reading from . . ./ GLORY TO YOU, LORD	Respond/ Gesture (Cross)			

This is the gospel . . ./ PRAISE TO YOU . . .	Respond		#48 use of dialogue
Homily	Listen/Sit	The living voice of the church helps us discover the always-new meaning of the word.	#36 use of visuals
		Homily/explanation of the word of God	#24 homilist
		(Catechist or adult other than the priest may speak to the children.)	#37 silence after homily
		(Song, if only one reading is proclaimed.)	#46 song after homily
PROFESSION OF FAITH	Recite/Stand		#31 musical settings of creed
			#39, #49 use of Apostles' and Nicene creeds
General intercessions/ RESPONSE	Respond (Sing)	The community asks God's help for those who are in need.	#36 visuals and general intercessions
			#22, #29 children's participation in intercessions

* elements in CAPITAL LETTERS indicate participation by children

† required elements *italicized*; suggested elements enclosed in parentheses

Considerations for Planners

The liturgy of the word must be short enough to control the children's interest and clear enough for them to grasp its message. Only one scripture reading, a gospel, is required (#42). Readings are selected according to the season and may be "cautiously" edited (#43) to simplify the proclamation for children. Brief commentaries, reading scripture in "parts," and other ways of making the scripture clear are recommended (#47). Psalm verses should be carefully selected, not overly long, and should be sung (#46).

The homily should receive special attention and preparation; dialogues are helpful (#47, 48); an adult other than the priest may take this responsibility (#24). Dramatic elements such as a slide presentation or dramatization of a reading may be done in a lively spirit, but should not distract from the dignity of the word of God or the atmosphere of worship. Noncommunicants may be dismissed before the creed, following the custom of the early church.

If a profession of faith is included, the Apostles' Creed may be used (#39). If intercessions are used, they should be written and presented by the children.

- How many and which reading(s) will be used?
- Who will proclaim the reading(s)?
- How will the reading(s) be proclaimed? (Drama, choral reading, with parts, introductory comments?)
- What form will response to a first reading take? (Responsorial psalm, silence, meditative music, choral reading, dance?)
- How and by whom will the children be helped to understand the reading(s)? (Homily, dialogue, dance, drama, choral presentation, visuals, explanatory or parallel reading from other literature?)
- Will the children make an act of faith? (Apostles' Creed, Nicene Creed, song, ritual?)
- How and by whom will the intercessions be created? What form will they take?
- Has some kind of physical action or involvement been included in this part of the Mass?
- Review the plans made to this point. Do they, taken as a whole, tend to complicate or to simplify the Mass?

Liturgy of the Eucharist

Purpose

To share in Jesus' eternal prayer of praise and thanksgiving; to bless and share the bread and wine in accordance with his command to "do this in memory of me"; to offer the eucharistic sacrifice and so "proclaim the death of the Lord until he comes."

Preparation of the Altar and Gifts

Ritual Elements*	Children's Action	Spirit of the Action	Elements of Masses with Children†	DMC References
Procession with gifts	Silence or Song	Instrumental music is also appropriate at this time. Before beginning the eucharistic action we prepare the altar. The bread and wine represent all that we have received from God and nurtured with our work: it will be returned to us—transformed. A collection for the poor and the church is taken up at this time and may be presented with the bread and wine.	*Bread and wine are placed on the altar.*	#18, #22 children's participation in procession with gifts #34 procession with gifts
Blessed are you . . ./ BLESSED BE GOD FOREVER	Respond	Simple prayers modeled on Jewish blessings. The priest says them quietly if there is song or other music.		
Pray, brethren . . ./ MAY THE LORD ACCEPT . . .	Respond	We pray that the Lord will accept the prayer, and offering, which is to follow, and that we will enjoy the fullness of its blessing.		
Prayer over the gifts/AMEN	Listen/Respond			

---

* elements in CAPITAL LETTERS indicate participation by children   † required elements *italicized;* suggested elements enclosed in parentheses

Considerations for Planners

The preparation of the altar and gifts should not be ignored—it is an important sign of the value God places on us and our work.

The *Directory* is silent on the manner in which this preparation is to be done. Planners should take their cue from the *Directory*'s comments on the more central actions of the Mass (liturgy of the word, eucharistic prayer, communion rite): they are to be simplified so that they are more accessible to children.

The approach to the preparation of the altar and gifts, then, should be the same. It is already a simple and straightforward rite, not a time for elaboration and fanfare. (See "An Overview of the Mass" by Gabe Huck.) The bread and wine are to be brought to the altar; everything is made ready for the great prayer which is to follow.

• Who and what will be involved in the procession? Can the children help make the altar ready in some way? Will the action be enhanced by song, or will song be a distraction? (Music, silence, dance, procession?)

• Will the priest acknowledge the gifts in a special way?

Liturgy of the Eucharist

Eucharistic Prayer

Ritual Elements*	Children's Action	Spirit of the Action	Elements of Masses with Children†	DMC References
			(Children give reasons for praising God.)	#22 children may add reasons for praise
INTRODUCTORY DIALOGUE	Stand/Respond	The eucharistic prayer begins with a dialogue which invites us to enter into this great prayer of thanksgiving.	*Introductory dialogue*	#39 use of responses #12 catechesis on the eucharist
Eucharistic prayer begins	Listen	The preface sets the tone of praise; it recalls some of the wonderful things the Father has done for us—the reasons for our praise. The preface varies with the occasion or season.	*Eucharistic Prayer with acclamations* (Use of eucharistic prayers for Masses with children.)	#23 priest's gestures #52 manner of proclamation
HOLY, HOLY, HOLY	Sing	This song of praise is based on Isaiah. The community adds its voice to the praise of God.	The first eucharistic prayer for children (EPC I) uses portions of the Holy as acclamations before the entire Holy is sung.	#30 singing acclamations #31 musical settings of Holy
Eucharistic prayer continues	Listen	The prayer continues with praise, invocation of the Holy Spirit and words of institution.	EPCs use the same words of institution as other eucharistic prayers.	The introduction to the EPCs calls attention to the following: #33 use of gestures

Let us proclaim . . ./ MEMORIAL ACCLAMATION	Sing	The community sings one of several alternative acclamations of the "mystery of faith."	The placement of this acclamation is changed in the EPCs in order to make its meaning clearer. In EPC III the priest proclaims the memorial of salvation; the children's acclamations are more general words of praise.	#23 festive nature of celebration #18 roles for children #19 Masses with adults #22 active participation #36 use of visuals
Eucharistic prayer continues	Listen	The priest continues the prayer with words of offering, and prayer for the unity and welfare of Christians living and dead.	EPC II and III include acclamations during this portion of the prayer.	
Through him, with him . . ./ AMEN	Sing	In the doxology, the concluding praise, we add our *fiat* to the sacrifice of Jesus and of the church. This is the most important "amen" of the Mass.		

* elements in CAPITAL LETTERS indicate participation by children   †required elements *italicized;* suggested elements enclosed in parentheses

Considerations for Planners

This prayer is the most important prayer of the entire Mass, but is usually the most tedious part of the Mass for children. It is long; there is little action between the procession with the gifts and the sign of peace.

To counter this, the church provides three eucharistic prayers for children (EPC), all of which are punctuated frequently with acclamations. Although the eucharistic prayer is proclaimed by the priest, it is prayed in the name of the whole church. With the acclamations the assembly adds its voice to the prayer. The burden falls on the priest to offer this prayer slowly and reverently, so that its importance will be apparent (#52).

The eucharistic prayers include, with varying degrees of emphasis, the following elements: affirmation of God's saving actions; a plea for the Holy Spirit to bless our gifts (epiclesis); the words of institution; remembrance of Jesus' passion, death and resurrection (anamnesis/memorial); the offering of Christ as our sacrifice; a remembrance of the needs of the church. It always ends with the doxology ("Through him, with him . . .") and elevation of the bread and wine.

• Which eucharistic prayer will be used? Why? Any commentary?
• Which acclamations will be used?
• Will there be any movement during this part of the Mass? Any gestures? Will the children be invited to stand nearer the altar?

Liturgy of the Eucharist

Communion Rite

Ritual Elements*	Children's Action	Spirit of the Action	Elements of Masses with Children†	DMC References
LORD'S PRAYER	Speak (Sing)	The preparation for communion begins with the most highly treasured Christian prayer.	Lord's Prayer	#53 rites before communion #23 introduction to the Lord's Prayer
Deliver us . . ./	Listen	The "deliver us" is an embolism—an elaboration of the petitions of the Lord's Prayer.		
FOR THE KINGDOM . . .	Respond (Sing)	We conclude the Lord's Prayer with words of praise.		
SIGN OF PEACE	Gesture	We reaffirm our unity in Christ.		
Breaking of the bread		The breaking of the bread is one of the key actions of the Mass: we who are many are made one body in Christ. If communion is under both forms, the wine is poured into cups for communion at this time.	Breaking of the bread	#31 musical settings of Lamb of God
LAMB OF GOD	Respond (Sing)	The Lamb of God accompanies the breaking of the bread. This litany is sung for as long as the breaking of the bread lasts.		#31 music settings of Lamb of God

This is the Lamb of God.../ LORD I AM NOT WORTHY...	Respond	We respond to the invitation to communion with a prayer of humility and hope.	*Invitation to communion*	
COMMUNION PROCESSION	Process/Receive communion	We receive the body and blood of Christ.	*Communion procession*	#34 communion procession
COMMUNION SONG	Sing		*Communion song, if possible*	#54 manner of receiving communion
				#22 communion as high point of participation
SILENT REFLECTION		A time of quiet for reflection and prayer.		#37 reflection after communion
Prayer after communion/AMEN	Listen/Respond	A prayer of petition that we may benefit from the eucharist we have received.		

* elements in CAPITAL LETTERS indicate participation by children

† required elements *italicized*; suggested elements enclosed in parentheses

Considerations for Planners

Draw special attention to the Lord's Prayer. It should be recited in an *unhurried* way, or sung. Young children enjoy executing gestures with this prayer.

Gestures other than a random handshake can be used for the peace greeting if they are a more natural sign of unity among the children.

Children's enthusiasm is heightened as they join the procession to the altar, usually singing a song that is well known to them. The song should be one that will help prepare them to receive communion in a spirit of reverence and understanding. The procession should not be rushed or chaotic. Catechists and parents will do more for the children by offering them the example of peacefully walking in procession than by busily directing traffic.

The cup may be offered to the children. Their catechesis and experience of the Mass should not omit this important element.

If a period of silent reflection is to be observed after communion, it should be introduced by a few words of commentary to help the children direct their thoughts. Properly handled, this will focus the children's attention on the meaning of the eucharist and prevent them from looking upon the communion as a sign that "Mass is almost over—hooray!"

- Will a peace sign be used? Why? What form will it take? (Song, gesture, dance?)
- What music will be used for the prayers, acclamations, procession and periods of silence?
- What will take place after communion? (Song, drama, dance, choral reading, commentary, silent reflection, prayer after communion?)

Concluding Rites

Purpose
To provide the liturgy with a gracious ending; to offer the celebrants a transition into their daily routine.

Ritual Elements*	Children's Action	Spirit of the Action	Elements of Masses with Children†	DMC References
			(The introduction to the blessing, "Bow your heads . . . ," may be expanded to relate the celebration to daily life.)	#54 relating the liturgy to daily life
Blessing/AMEN	Respond/Gesture	The final blessing has simple and elaborate forms. It always concludes with the trinitarian blessing.	*Blessing in the name of the Trinity*	#54 final blessing
Dismissal/ THANKS BE TO GOD	Respond	We are reminded to live according to the word we have received.		
CLOSING SONG	Sing			

* elements in CAPITAL LETTERS indicate participation by children   † required elements *italicized*; suggested elements enclosed in parentheses

Considerations for Planners
The conclusion should not be a letdown, an afterthought or an anticlimax. Without prolonging the liturgy it should offer a ceremonious closing. If ministers leave the area, it should be done in the same measured and dignified way they entered. If a closing hymn is sung, it should be lively and well known by the congregation.

- How will the spirit of the celebration be maintained until the end? (Song, commentary, ritual, procession?)
- Review the plans you have made to this point. Do they, taken as a whole, tend to complicate or to simplify the Mass? Are you introducing too many "good things" at once? Will the parts of the celebration flow into one another naturally? Can you simplify it even more?

V. For Presiders & Other Grown-ups

Getting to Know You

— Elizabeth McMahon Jeep

At a children's Mass not long ago, my eight-year-old son leaned over during the homily and said, "Mom! He's talking to us like we're kindergarten kids!" He was right. The tone of voice, the delivery and message of the homily were totally inappropriate for the six- to eight-year-olds gathered there with their families. It was a great shame: the priest had obviously spent time preparing the homily, yet he left the children with a sense of condescension rather than inspiration.

If this were an isolated case there would be no point in writing this article, but it happens often enough to be considered routine. In fact, many priests shy away from children's liturgies precisely because they suspect that they cannot "speak the language" of children. And, unfortunately, those priests who do seek the help of teachers or religion coordinators are often dismissed with a casual, "Just keep it short, Father, and you'll do OK."

For the most part, Father is not doing OK. He is as ill-at-ease in the presence of young children as he would be in the darkest reaches of the Amazon rain forest. Young people are a strange and alien tribe to him: apprentice human beings without feelings or insight, cute but unpredictable, the object of benevolent apprehension. And why not? The bachelor lifestyle of the rectory has been designed to eliminate the distractions of family life. There is no patter of little feet in the kitchen, no roller skates in the hall, no prom dress in the closet. It is not surprising that many priests do not know a Lego from a Yoda.

Whatever its virtues, there is a danger that the protection from family obligations which celibacy offers can backfire and isolate the priest from the people he was ordained to serve. It does not reduce the symbolism and importance of celibacy to admit that it imposes upon each priest an obligation to create his own contacts and relationships with children and other nonclerics.

What can a priest do, then, to break through this barrier and get to know more about children? Obviously, one cannot learn about children from a distance, from a book or from hearsay—but only through actual and continuing contact. It is essential to have some child-friends. It is hard to establish this one-on-one relationship in a classroom where 20 or so children want to share your attention. The religion classroom also imposes a great deal of restraint (law, order and politeness) on the children's responses. Besides, what is needed is an opportunity to listen, not to teach.

Try, then, for a setting where you are not exercising a ministerial role: friendship can only develop where both parties are participating freely. The situation should throw you and the child or children together long enough to get beyond the polite stage. You could, for example, babysit for a couple who will be away for a whole day, or several days. You could take some nieces and nephews for a day at an amusement park. Running an art or sports program can be helpful if your time with the children is unhurried and unharried, if the group contains both girls and boys, and if you allow the relationship to grow beyond concern for the task at hand.

A satisfactory initial experience can be arranged by inviting a few children to help you with a specific task, such as folding and stuffing the parish bulletin, some useful job that will allow for quiet conversation. Meet with the children again, make it a point to recognize and greet them whenever you go to the school or CCD area, take them for a treat, deliver them to their homes and meet their parents. In short, develop some "particular friendships."

While you are enjoying their visit, try to notice as much about the children as you can. Later, try to clarify your observations. List three things they seem to know a lot about. What did they do with their hands, feet and bodies during the conversation? What were you talking about when they seemed to be listening attentively? What time of day was it? Were they comfortable? Pleased to be included?

By listening to children, by dealing with them directly and not always through the agency of another adult, a priest can gradually learn their language, become comfortable and relaxed around them, discover some of their needs and fears, develop a sensitivity to their feelings and interests, and, most important, develop a taste for their companionship. The results are worth the effort: there is refreshment and delight in the companionship of children. Their responses can keep you alert because they are usually very direct and uncomplicated. Do not ask them what they thought of your homily, for example, unless you want an honest answer!

Children generally take the first step in offering trust, giving you the benefit of every doubt, refraining from analysis or judgment. In return, they impose only modest expectations on you. They require trust, respect, honesty and a certain degree of availability.

Another useful step in becoming realistic about children could involve organizing and leading a large group through some kind of event. Whether you plan a picnic, make puppets or visit the zoo together, the important thing is that you make all the arrangements and remain in charge from beginning to end. This means that you present and explain the activity to the children, reserve the space, make the name tags, order the supplies, recruit the adult helpers, stay around until the last bag of trash is carried away and conduct follow-up activities. No one who has done this will ever again deal with children as an abstraction, or accept generalizations: "All first graders like animals," "Girls like art; boys like sports," "Children are cute."

But more important than this, you will have begun to experience the feeling of being a *leader* of children. You will begin to understand why it is so difficult to act as presider at a liturgy you have had no part in planning, among children you do not know. You will begin to sense that the preparations for an event are an important part of children's experience of it. (Q: What did you like most about the visit to the zoo? A: The seats on the bus were red and bouncy.) You will begin to realize that children experience liturgy as a complex of sights, sounds, movements, weather, color, the interplay of repetition and surprise—*not* as an arrangement of words and ideas. You will begin to grasp the physicalness of children.

And as a bonus, you will have an opportunity to seek the advice, guidance and cooperation of other members of the parish staff who are more accustomed than you to dealing with children *en groupe*. Nothing disarms a person and deepens respect like being asked for advice!

The main task of childhood is growth. Children are the group within society that is most likely to be maturing, changing for the better, learning through repetition and recognition of mistakes, becoming more competent, more aware, more knowledgeable. The people, therefore, who will feel most comfortable with children and who can offer them the most help, are those who are aware of their own growth. Such people are not likely to be defensive or pompous or distant: they are likely to be good listeners, good learners. They are likely to be humble enough to live well with children.

It is easy for a priest to get trapped into playing a role that is not his own: acting out the projections of other people, trying to imitate the priest before him "who was so good with the children." But it will be more satisfactory for all concerned if you keep trying to discover what it means for *you* to become a pastor to children. A pastor is one who knows the territory well enough to guide the flock to nourishing grass and pure water. A pastor is one who leads, but does not force or cajole or manipulate. A pastor is one who walks along with, rather than trying to give directions from a distance. Almost anyone who does his homework can be a good pastor/presider for children. It is not a matter of playing the guitar or taking summer courses in liturgy or of changing your personality. Being a pastor is a service you can offer, not a role you must play or a personality you must adopt. As Shakespeare wrote, "It is a wise father that knows his own child." It is a wise priest who sets himself diligently to that task.

The Priest as Storyteller

— Elizabeth McMahon Jeep

Have you ever pictured yourself sitting in the smoky darkness of a cave, wrapped in bearskins, filling the evening shadows with your stories? Actually there is a great similarity between the role of priest in the Catholic community and that of storyteller in an ancient tribe. Each bears official responsibility for handing on the stories which tell of the group's history and its uniqueness, its folk wisdom and its vision of the future. They tell the people who they are, how they came to be a people and how they are related to other peoples. Storytellers teach the young what the community holds dear, and what it expects of them. And finally, their stories continually renew the hopes which give shape and direction to the communal life.

In ancient times the followers of the Lord, whether in exile or at home, gathered around their teachers and elders for the retelling, reaffirmation and reliving of their covenant. From this ritual the liturgy of the word has evolved, precisely as an occasion for retelling the mighty deeds of our God and our formation as his holy people. But these tribal stories cannot be handed on in an aloof or objective way. The ceremony calls for the active engagement of the listeners; they enter into each story and relive it through song and prayer and acceptance of the invitation it contains to share in the covenant. This process is one of the ways in which the eucharist plays its part in the gradual initiation of children into the faith community. Indeed, the priest's skill as a storyteller is never more evident than when he acts as celebrant of a liturgy with children.

This sounds like pretty exciting stuff. Why, then, is the liturgy of the word (and other rites patterned on it) so often more of a problem than a pleasure? Why do we feel compelled to dress it up to make it palatable for children? Surely, if anyone in the community loves a good story, it is the children. They delight in hearing a tale if it is new and savor it even more if it is familiar. Unlike adults, children do not listen for logic or for new information. They listen, first of all, for a good story—a story that has power, but also a story that echoes in their own experience or imagination. In his thought-provoking study, *The Uses of Enchantment*, Bruno Bettleheim shows that it is not merely the adventure and imaginativeness of the fairy tales that make them so attractive to children, but the fact that each one tells something hopeful about working through a difficult aspect of life. Children (and most adults) are seldom aware that listening to the story of "Snow White" or "The Twelve Dancing Princesses" is helping them prepare for a time when they will have to leave the shelter of home. By imagining themselves into the heroine's place, the listeners absorb the heroine's courage, cleverness or other virtues.

Is there, then, some flaw in our stories? Hardly! No other book on earth can compare to the Bible for stories of adventure and

76

miracle, banishment and battle, for dramatic confrontations with evil, for heroes and devils and valiant women. Rather, it is our storytelling skills that need improvement. Storytelling is, after all, a living art, a performing art, much like music. Does the pianist hand out printed copies of the score and let the concert patrons read along? Heaven forbid! The audiences would get the impression that the artist had no confidence in his or her own ability to hold their attention. Besides, the music will take on a new form of existence when it is played, and it is the performed music into which the pianist wants the listeners to enter. The music's power to move and excite can be ascribed both to the skill of the musician and to the brilliance of the composer. In the same way, the one who proclaims God's word must bring it to life at each liturgical event. The word must, again and again, be made flesh in order to dwell among us. This charism is akin to the gift of prophecy and it finds explanation in the theology of incarnation, but those studies would carry us beyond the scope of this article. It is sufficient simply to note here that both story and storyteller have a contribution to make to the power of the liturgical experience.

Each concert is an unrepeatable event for which the pianist must diligently prepare. Just so must the priest prepare himself for the double storytelling in the liturgy of the word: the proclamation of the gospel and the presentation of the homily. The preparation, both as a long-range program and as immediate background for each celebration, is threefold.

Take Yourself Seriously

The presbyter is always interested in improving his technical skills because the effectiveness of his ministry depends to a large extent on his professional performance. Obviously a good storyteller cannot have a voice like sandpaper, cannot mumble, cannot lace each sentence with "y'know" or "okay?" A professional liturgist learns the techniques of breath control, voice projection, variation of tone and mood, and

the other skills that people who use their voices professionally need to know. For some a course in drama or elocution could be helpful. Others might want to listen to a tape of their voices. Certainly, listening to people who deal with children every day, such as librarians, teachers, parents and puppeteers, would be useful. The best style to develop is one with which you are comfortable, aiming for a voice that is animated without being condescending, suited to the sanctuary not the stage, and that draws its strength from inner conviction rather than gimmicks.

Take the Story Seriously

Ruth Sawyer writes in *The Way of the Storyteller* that good storytellers have an intense urge to share with others what has moved them deeply. The words of the Bible must come to life first in the heart of the speaker, then they can take possession of the listener, especially the young listener. It is not easy for a busy parish priest to take time to meditate on the reading(s) which will be proclaimed at the children's Mass. Yet many make that effort. It is possible for a priest who has a natural way with children to get along with a minimum of preparation. He is able to make a reading vivid without advance notice. He is able to deliver an instant homily or engage the children in "dialogue." While these men may succeed in engaging the children's attention, they are seldom able to offer real nourishment. They draw the children to themselves but not necessarily to the Lord Jesus.

Far more helpful are the priest-presiders for whom liturgy is a high priority: preparation is felt as a real obligation. They are the men who attend the liturgy planning sessions so that they can add their own insights, but also so that they can hear the reflections and discussion among the children and their teachers. The first stage in preparation for the storyteller, then, is to listen to the listeners, to learn what ideas and experiences the children will bring to their meeting with the word.

Selection of the readings is one of the most important tasks of the planning committee.

Children cannot possibly respond to three readings at once. We can all learn from the children's librarians that one good story, carefully prepared and properly told, is better than two. *Directory for Masses with Children* (#41–45) wisely suggests reducing the number of readings at a children's liturgy. It also notes that planners are not limited to the selections contained in the lectionary. When more than one reading is to be used, then, they should be selected as a pair, with one containing a vivid image or narrative and the other being a short commentary on its meaning. One reading will, of course, always be taken from the gospel.

Next the storyteller edits the passage for the age and background of the children with whom he will celebrate. He is careful to preserve the power and style of the original and above all, to avoid slipping into a "childish manner of speech" (as the *Directory* puts it). The lectionaries for children published by the Pueblo Publishing Company show how a reading can be edited for children without losing its scriptural integrity.

Take Children Seriously

They are capable of prayer—childish prayer, but true prayer nevertheless. They are capable of worship. They are, in fact, natural liturgists because they are still very close to nature; they love rituals, and they adore stories! For children, gospel stories are fresh and new, filled with the same power and surprise that they held for the first generation of Christians. We can, therefore, approach the readings without apology.

The storyteller-celebrant is only half-finished when the gospel proclamation has been well prepared. Next he develops a homily to help the children realize the connection between the gospel story and their life stories. To do this well a priest must understand both the meaning of the scriptural passage in terms of God's relationship with his people and the contemporary situation of his child listeners. How and where does this story and the lives of these people converge? What is the connection? If he does not have any realistic experiences with children, or knowledge of their habits and hopes and fears to draw from, the homilist may resort to superficial lessons and pious moralizing. While children cannot follow adult theologizing, they can be helped to discover God's presence and action in their lives. It is that help that the homilist tries to give.

Scripture and listeners and skills are to be taken seriously, but they should not be thought of as burdensome or grim. Storytelling is a joyful, beneficial, satisfying art to pursue, and anyone who works closely with children cannot help but experience life as direct and lighthearted. Children can sense the attitude of a presider who enjoys being with them and sharing in their liturgy. They do not ask that he be an entertainer, Big Bird or another Danny Kaye. Rather they look for an adult who appreciates them and shares his insights with them. Such a storyteller will always find a good audience gathered around his campfire.

Homilies for Children

— Elizabeth McMahon Jeep

Paul was quite a preacher. In Troas so many people crowded in to hear him that they were sitting on the windowsills. Good as he was, however, he just could not keep the young people awake, and before you knew it a lad named Eutychus nodded off, tumbled out the window and fell three stories to the ground. Capturing the children's attention has not gotten any easier over the past 19 centuries. In fact, if windowsills had not been eliminated from our churches we would undoubtedly have lost a goodly number of young worshipers by now. Are there more creative solutions to this particular problem of worship?

Although some excellent preaching is being directed toward children, remarkably little has been written on this subject. The *Directory for Masses with Children* merely states that the homily should be given "great prominence," that it may sometimes take the form of a dialogue, and that it may be given by someone better at speaking with children than is the presider. This leaves the priest who wishes to improve his skills with little to go on but ingenuity and the ideas he can pick up from his friends. Perhaps a brief "state of the art" message may be of help.

Parish Masses with Children Present

One can speak to children directly without violating the essentially adult character of the Sunday liturgy in three ways: (1) address a brief postscript to them at the end of the main homily; (2) direct the first section of the homily to them and add a second part for the adults; (3) offer the children a separate liturgy of the word.

The first of these methods is perhaps the simplest to implement. On the feast of the Holy Family, for example, the homilist can speak to the adults on the family as model of the relationship we all have with one another in Jesus Christ. Then he can say, "I will now speak to all of the children here this morning. Will all of you please listen to me for one minute?" This announcement gives the children a chance to gather their wandering minds and to stop squirming. After a few words about people's desire to give gifts to those they love, he can ask the children to think of the most excellent gift that they could wish for their parents. After a period of silence, so that they can think, the priest asks them to whisper to their parents, if they are present, what their wish for them is. End of homily. These remarks to the children are always brief, simple and action-oriented. Sometimes it will be important to mention an age group specifically: "Will all of the children twelve and under whisper. . . ." This sort of conclusion constitutes a true homily, for it flows from the readings and seasons. This method is suitable for almost any situation and does not require a designated "family Mass."

The second method is similar but more difficult. The homilist speaks to the children,

79

at the same time laying the foundation for the message he will direct toward the adults. For example, the readings for the Fifth Sunday of Lent (cycle A) contain Ezekiel's prophecy regarding the dry bones, and an account of the raising of Lazarus. The children's homily centers on the similarity of the dry bones to Pinocchio, who began as a wooden puppet but came to life when he started acting in a thoughtful, considerate manner. Similarly, the life Jesus offers is more than a matter of breathing and outgrowing sweaters. Both children and adults can grasp this so far; now the preacher draws the adults one step further, "Do you know anyone who is deadwood? Anyone who is walking mechanically through life? Do you know of a marriage that is dead, or has robot-like aspects to it? Do you know a person whose hopes are dead? You may know one such person very well, know how death and life can struggle within. Jesus says, 'I am the resurrection and the life.'"

In this second model the homily for each group has the same message; the adults are merely asked to discover its truth in their own experiences. This approach is especially useful on special occasions such as first communion, where children are the "main event" and yet do not comprise the entire assembly. When it is not possible to draw from a given set of readings a message that is relevant to both adults and children, the first model can be used.

The third model, the separate liturgy of the word, is quite popular in some parts of Europe: many parish plants have been designed with a children's assembly room close to the main church. The value of this method is, of course, its flexibility. Children can be given more of the ministerial roles. The homily can take the form of dialogue, drama, art, creative writing, mime, music or film.

Lack of appropriate space only partly explains the disinterest Americans have shown for this approach, except for a brief period during the late 1960s. We also have a fear (perhaps exaggerated) that children will become a separate community if they are not integrated with the adults during the entire eucharist. Of course, the separate liturgy of the word exacts a high price: someone must plan the presentation of the readings, edit them judiciously, choose the psalm, select songs and gestures and rituals or other activities. Musicians are needed, and a number of facilitators proportionate to the number of children participating. Enthusiasm for putting that kind of planning and effort into the Sunday eucharist has waned. Sometimes catechists involved in planning these liturgies have given them a more educational or social than liturgical direction. Then, too, some have opposed the idea (despite the specific recommendation of this approach in the *Directory* #17), questioning the legitimacy of bilocating the celebration and having more than one presider.

Children's Masses

The Mass which is planned specifically for children presents an entirely different situation. There the priest may direct the homily with greater precision and may draw upon the wide range of options mentioned above, so that he will be able to speak to the children in a medium that they can understand.

The presider has an important resource that is almost entirely neglected. The *Directory* suggests that, with the consent of the pastor, an adult other than the presider may speak to the children after the gospel. Certainly at times the catechist will have the insight and the time to prepare the homily; on other occasions a parent with a new infant might speak to the children about calling God "our Father"; a blind person could speak on the beauty of creation in sound and touch and smell and movement; a mime might offer a nonverbal homily, an approach especially appropriate for young children whose minds are still more intuitive than logical. Anyone who gives a homily must meet the same high standards of preparation and presentation that the priest is accustomed to meet. In other words, any who share in this ministry must know what they are doing, and not just act as a living "show and tell.'' The homily is always a meeting of the scriptures and life.

Priests most often use the "dialogue homily" at children's liturgies. This is easy to do, and it wisely involves the children verbally, if not physically. As a technique, however, it is generally misunderstood and greatly overrated. First, true dialogue is impossible with a whole roomful of children you know only marginally. Second, most of the questions used to initiate the "dialogue" are so obvious that older children are embarrassed to answer. The homilist who does ask a thought-provoking question ("What does that mean?"; "On what occasion might Jesus make that same statement today?") risks an unexpected answer, and generally will have to call on other children until one gives the answer expected, thus allowing the homily to continue. A truly conversational homily can be an exciting experience for children and homilist, but the number of occasions when it can be done well are extremely limited.

This does not mean we cannot develop other, more satisfactory ways of involving the children verbally. Black preachers, for example, know how to invite the listeners to add their "amens" to the homily as it goes along: "Do you believe that Jesus raised Lazarus? Then say, 'amen!' Do you believe that Jesus will raise you also? Then say, 'amen!'" We could perhaps use some of this back-and-forth style.

Final Thoughts

1. Keep it short! The work of one homilist who presides at monthly SPRED (Special Religious Education Division, archdiocese of Chicago) Masses is a model for us all; they are *one sentence*, repeated slowly, personally, with dignity, three times. Of course hours of planning and prayer plus three weeks of catechetical preparation have brought the children and adults, their catechists and their presider to the moment when that word is spoken. As in everything important, quality not quantity is the soul of good homiletics.

2. Draw your message from the readings.

3. Speak a strengthening word to the children. Raise them up, encourage the good in them, verify their special place and role in God's love; support their attempts at generosity, honesty, family loyalty; invite their involvement in faith and prayer. This does not mean that you paint a picture of life as always happy, upbeat, superficial, but that you help them to recognize and name their fears, sorrows and problems. Share with them your own hope and confidence in the Jesus who heals, loves and leads.

4. Again, make it short! If you can't say it in ten sentences, you certainly won't say it in 20.

5. Avoid childish language or teen jargon. These are the languages of the family or the peer group, and not appropriate for an outsider to use. No useful purpose is served when you speak of "mummies and daddies," for example, even to kindergarten children.

6. Remember poor Eutychus, and keep it short!

The Liturgy and "Memorizable" Prayers

— Elizabeth McMahon Jeep

There are many times when we wish to reach back into memory for a prayer, something majestic to match a sunset, perhaps, or something with which to respectfully plead a cause, or something penitential to say by heart while straightening out a mess we have created. There are times, when waiting for the light to change or putting away groceries, that I ask my memory to supply some beginning of praise or reflection, but it fails. Not that I never learned anything by heart; on the contrary, I learned my school prayers too well. They drown out all that I have tried to learn as an adult. They are filled with "hoopskirted" phrases concerning "deep affection and grief of soul," and "casting myself upon my knees" and "sweetest" Jesus who will "quench the devouring flames" with "a few drops of his most precious blood." It is the overblown language of Victorian sentiment, more likely to provoke and awareness of one's age than an awareness of the presence and power of God.

No doubt many readers who use a form of the liturgy of the hours in their daily prayer have had a chance as adults to memorize the great phrases and attitudes of the psalms and are unaware of the culture gap we layfolk experience.

What will the next generation of students say about their school prayers? Will they rise up 20 years from now to criticize us for giving them, too, a diet of weak-kneed prayers, full of trendy jargon and self-conscious posturing?

Or will they complain that they have learned nothing by heart because we never used the same prayer twice? Or will they thank us for introducing them gradually to the strong and nourishing words of praise that are a part of our religious patrimony.

The teacher, religious educator or parent who wishes to enrich a child's memory bank of prayers can do no better than follow the example set by the liturgy. There, for example, a psalm verse is used as an antiphon or chorus for the meditation after the reading of scripture. These antiphons alone are a suitable beginning for our youngest students, whether they are gathered in a classroom or around a dinner table, and can be repeated often enough for the children to learn by heart. The middle children can learn Sunday's antiphon by using it as a refrain each day during the following (or preceding) week, as the teacher weaves together appropriate meditations composed of other psalms, other passages from scripture, or original meditations based on the material being studied. Older children might learn longer passages, especially if they are put to music, edited slightly for choral reading, or tailored to fit the modes of prayer most helpful to children at various stages of their religious development. (In recognizing the special help that music offers to memory, we might pay more attention to singing our daily prayer, and we might also closely monitor the lyric portions of the catechetical songs we teach.)

82

Once we learn to "raid" the liturgy for memorizable prayer forms and fragments, we discover that liturgy itself is a model which any good prayer might imitate. The *language* of liturgy is measured, theologically appropriate, filled with poetry and symbol yet never far from human experience. It offers a catalogue of attitudes: thanksgiving, awe, petition, mourning, trust, penitence. Liturgy also offers a variety of *rhythms*: the repetition of the "Lord, have mercy," the alternation of voices in a litany, the quiet faith or joyous praise of various acclamations, the dignified pace of a creed, or the steady march of a preface building up to the shout of "Hosanna!"

The many structures and changes within the church's official prayer (and let us remember that "liturgy" includes the rites of anointing, initiation and reconciliation; the liturgy of the hours; various eucharistic prayers and propers; and seasonal feasts) offer a *methodology* as well as an anthology of memorizable prayers. The method includes bodily movement by design and not by accident. The standing, sitting, kneeling, anointing, bowing, processing, candle lighting, bread breaking, hand holding, signing with crosses, blessing with water, lifting of arms—all *are* prayer, not a mere physical accompaniment to prayer. These gestures are important in private as well as communal worship.

The liturgical method is also a blend and balance of repetition and variety. There must be enough routine in the use of word or ritual to allow each person to participate comfortably, without undue distraction from commentators and directors. But at the same time there must be some surprise so that each celebration is clearly experienced as unique and significant, not the merely mechanical fulfillment of a prescribed routine.

As a praying community we can look back over two decades of renewal and say, "We've come a long way, baby!" The most significant change has probably been a growing capacity to nourish our prayer with scripture. We are becoming "a people of the Book." We are also moving toward a more fundamental understanding of the dynamic of liturgy, and are discovering the unique relationship between learning to celebrate well as part of the community and learning to pray well as individual believers.

Copyrights and Wrongs

The Copyright Law

Q. Why is there a copyright law?

A. United States copyright laws stem from Article 1, Section 8 of the Constitution. Our forebears determined that it was in the public interest that the creation of a person's mind and spirit should, under law, belong for a limited time to that person or, if deceased, to the family of that person. The law is designed to encourage the development of the arts and sciences by protecting the work of the creative individuals in our society.

Q. What is a copyright?

A. A copyright is a statutory grant of certain rights for a limited time.

Q. When is a work copyrighted?

A. A work is protected from the moment of creation, fixed in a copy or phonorecord.

Q. Who owns a copyright?

A. The composer and lyricist, or the duly authorized agent (publisher) to whom they have transferred ownership.

Portions of ''Copyrights and Wrongs'' are taken from *Copyright: The United States Copyright Law, A Guide for Church Musicians,* a booklet produced by the Church Music Publishers Association. No copyright is claimed in the booklet. You are encouraged to reproduce ''Copyrights and Wrongs'' in order to assure the widest possible circulation.

Q. What are the exclusive rights of copyright owners?

A. To reproduce the copyright work in copies or phonorecords.

To prepare derivative works based upon the copyrighted work.

To distribute copies of the copyrighted work to the public by sale or other manner.

To perform the copyrighted work publicly.

To display the copyrighted work publicly.

Q. For how long is a copyright good?

A. Under the 1976 copyright law, works created after 1 January 1978 will be protected for the life of the composer or author plus 50 years. Works created prior to 1 January 1978, if renewed, will be protected for 75 years from the date copyright was originally secured.

Q. How do I know if something is copyrighted?

A. By law, copyrighted material should be marked with the copyright symbol, © (or the word *copyright*), the year of the copyright, and the owner of the copyright. For example, Copyright © 1982, Smith Publications. Beware, absence of a copyright notice does not necessarily mean that the material is free to use. Assume that any publication which bears a copyright notice of 1906 or later is protected by copyright. Any piece of music with a copyright of 1905 or earlier is in the public domain.

Q. What does public domain mean?
A. Something which is in the public domain belongs to the public. You have the right to reproduce any piece of music which is in the public domain. In these cases, see whether the lyrics are copyrighted separately. It is possible for the melody to be in the public domain, but the lyrics or accompaniment to be copyrighted. Check to be sure.

Q. Aren't churches and schools exempt from copyright provisions?
A. Absolutely not!

Q. Aren't there occasions in which educational institutions may reproduce copyrighted material without permission?
A. Yes, the current legislation specifies purposes for which reproduction of copyrighted material without permission of the copyright owner is allowed. This is to balance the rights of the copyright holder and the needs of a democratic public. This is known as fair use. The copyright law (#107) states:

> The fair use of a copyrighted work . . . for purposes such as criticism, comment, news reporting, teaching (including multiple copies for classroom use), scholarship, or research, is not an infringement of copyright. In determining whether the use of a work in any particular case is a fair use the factors to be considered shall include—
>
> 1. the purpose and character of the use, including whether such use is of a commercial nature or is for nonprofit educational purposes;
> 2. the nature of the copyrighted work;
> 3. the amount and substantiality of the portion used in relation to the copyrighted work as a whole; and
> 4. the effect of the use upon the potential market for or value of the copyrighted work.

Q. Wouldn't these fair use provisions include reproducing music or words for liturgy without prior permission of the copyright holder? Church schools are nonprofit institutions, and worship is not commercial in nature.
A. No, they do not. Music publishers and music educators were active participants in shaping the new copyright law. They have developed the following guidelines to clarify the fair use of music for educational purposes.

Guidelines for Educational Uses of Music

The purpose of these guidelines is to state the minimum, not the maximum, standards of educational fair use of copyrighted works. The conditions determining the extent of permissible copying under these guidelines may change in the future. Moreover, the following guidelines are not intended to limit the types of copying permitted under the standards of fair use stated in the copyright law.

1. *Permissible Use*
   a. Emergency copying to replace purchased copies which for any reason are not available for imminent performance provided purchased replacement copies shall be substituted in due course.
   b. For academic purposes, other than performance, single or multiple copies of excerpts of works may be made, provided that the excerpts do not comprise a part of the whole which would constitute a performable unit such as a section, movement or aria, but in no case more than ten percent of the whole work. The number of copies shall not exceed one copy per pupil.
   c. Printed copies which have been purchased may be edited or simplified provided that the fundamental character of the work is not distorted or the lyrics, if any, altered or lyrics added if none exist.

d. A single copy of recordings of performances by students may be made for evaluation or rehearsal purposes and may be retained by the educational institution or individual teacher.

e. A single copy of a sound recording (such as a tape, disc or cassette) of copyrighted music may be made from sound recordings owned by an educational institution or an individual teacher for the purpose of constructing aural exercises or examinations and may be retained by the educational institution or individual teacher. (This pertains only to the copyright of the music itself and not to any copyright which may exist in the sound recording.)

2. *Prohibitions*

a. Copying to create or replace or substitute for anthologies, compilations or collective works.

b. Copying of or from works intended to be "consumable" in the course of study or of teaching such as workbooks, exercises, standardized tests and answer sheets and like material.

c. Copying for the purpose of performance, except as in 1a above.

d. Copying for the purpose of substituting for the purchase of music, except as in 1a and 1b above.

e. Copying without inclusion of the copyright notice which appears on the printed copy.

3. *Performance*

Performance is one of the copyright owner's exclusive rights. The new law provides that *you may*:

a. perform nondramatic musical works or dramatico-musical works of a religious nature, in the course of services at places of worship or at a religious assembly.

b. perform a nondramatic musical work if there is no purpose of direct or indirect commerical advantage, no fee or compensation paid to the performers, promoters or organizers, and no admission charge; if there is an admission charge, all of the proceeds must be used only for educational or charitable purposes. The performance may not take place if the copyright owner objects in writing seven days before the performance.

c. perform a nondramatic musical work on closed circuit television to other classrooms or to disabled persons for teaching purposes, only if the transmission is part of the systematic activities of the church, and only if the performance is directly related and of material assistance to the teaching content of the program.

Q. Explain how this applies to liturgical music.

A. The music teacher or organist who buys one copy of music can play it at a not-for-profit public performance, such as a school or parish worship service. If enough copies are purchased for a choir to use, the choir may perform it at a worship service without further permission. But it is specifically *against the law* to buy one copy (or two or three) and then duplicate the piece for the rest of the choir or instrumentalists or congregation without permission of the copyright holder.

Q. Does this include the words as well as musical notation?

A. Yes, lyrics as well as music are protected by copyright.

Q. What are the penalties for breaking the copyright law?

A. The remedies provided by the law to a copyright owner could mean that churches or schools found making illegal copies, or otherwise infringing, could face:

1. Payment of from $250 to $10,000 (statutory damages) and if the court finds willfulness, up to $50,000 per infringement;
2. If willful infringement for commercial advantage and private financial gain is proved, fines of up to $50,000 and/or two years' imprisonment, or both.

The nature of the remedies provided by the law indicates that copyright infringement is something serious and needs to be viewed with concern.

Providing Legal Copies

Q. How can a school afford enough copies of music for the student body?

A. There are several considerations. First, how much music do children need to have? Much of the essential music for Masses—psalm responses, gospel alleluias, the acclamations of the eucharistic prayers—is best learned and performed by heart, without printed words or music. Because of their brevity, acclamations and responses are easily memorized. Because of their function in the Mass, it is better that the children respond to the action of the liturgy, and to the presider and music ministers, than occupy themselves by finding their place in a book or order of worship. For this music, a school would need a resource library, enough copies for the teachers, instrumentalists and choir, if any.

Second, the liturgial music used with school or religious education classes should lead the children to the experience of Sunday parish Mass. Children should not have an entirely different repertoire from the adults. While some music may be needed specifically for the children (the acclamations for the eucharistic prayers, for example), consider using the same basic source that is used by the parish at large. Encourage the parish to purchase hymnals that are well suited for all parish worship, including Masses with children.

Third, many schools regularly celebrate liturgies with only one class or grade level. The school may wish to purchase a quantity of music books for use by these smaller groups. When the entire student body gathers for liturgy, select music that is known by heart, that is available in the parish hymnal, or which you have permission to reproduce for that occasion.

Q. What are the procedures for getting permission to reprint copyrighted material?

A. (1) Find out who holds the copyright. This information will be noted either on the first page of each selection in a collection of songs, in the front of the book on the copyright page, or, in larger hymnals, with the acknowledgments.

(2) Write to the publisher or composer to request permission to reproduce the material. The publisher's address is usually on the copyright page. In your letter include the following: title of song(s) you wish to copy, name of composer(s) and/or lyricist(s), the number of copies you plan to reproduce, the occasion for which you will use the copies (e.g., a one-time occasion like confirmation, in a semipermanent hymnal).

(3) You will be notified whether the permission is granted and, if so, what conditions you must meet (fees, acknowledgments, etc.)

Q. Is it permissible to use overhead or slide transparencies to project words and music?

A. Yes, with the appropriate permission. Check the guidelines for fair use. If the use of projectors substitutes for the purchase of music for participants, it is not a legitimate reproduction of copyrighted material without the proper permission.

Q. May exclusive or sexist language be changed?

A. Ask. If you are requesting permission to reproduce lyrics and would like to alter the words, inquire about the lyrics and include the suggested change. Many composers have adjusted their lyrics because of sensitivity to exclusive language. The publisher may have a revised text.

Q. Is there any problem with reprinting scripture texts or parts of the Mass in a worship program?

A. The translations of the scriptures and the rites of the Mass and the other sacraments and official rites are copyrighted. You must have permission to reprint them in participation aids. It is not ordinarily a good idea to print the scripture readings or words of the prayers spoken by the priest or the responses which are known by heart. It is better for anyone, especially children, to listen to the scriptures and prayers than to give their attention to a book. If it is necessary to include scripture or prayer texts in an order of worship, write to the copyright holder for permission. The appropriate names and addresses are listed below.

Q. This all seems very complicated.

A. Think of music purchases and copyrights as permission to use someone else's property and the exercise of justice. Musicians deserve recompense for their work. We depend on their creativity for the enrichment of our common prayer. The copyright law establishes a climate in which the creative process can mature and thrive with equal protection for all.

For permission to reprint liturgical texts, the words of the prayers and acclamations found in the sacramentary or the rites, write to:

The International Commission on English in the Liturgy (ICEL)
1234 Massachusetts Avenue NW
Washington DC 20005

ICEL has established a policy for permission for one-time use of the liturgical texts as prepared by ICEL for use in the United States.

For permission to reprint scripture texts, write to the appropriate publisher:

The New American Bible
United States Catholic Conference
1312 Massachusetts Avenue NW
Washington DC 20005

The Jerusalem Bible
Doubleday and Company, Inc.
277 Park Avenue
New York NY 10017

The Revised Standard Version (Catholic Edition)
National Council of Churches
Division of Education and Ministry
475 Riverside Drive
New York NY 10115

The Grail Psalms
A. P. Watt Ltd.
26–28 Bedford Row
London WC1R 4HL
England